Cambridge El

Elements in New Religious Movements
edited by
Rebecca Moore
San Diego State University
Founding Editor
James R. Lewis
Wuhan University

THE TRANSCENDENTAL MEDITATION MOVEMENT

Dana Sawyer
Maine College of Art

Cynthia Humes
Claremont McKenna College

CAMBRIDGE
UNIVERSITY PRESS

Shaftesbury Road, Cambridge CB2 8EA, United Kingdom

One Liberty Plaza, 20th Floor, New York, NY 10006, USA

477 Williamstown Road, Port Melbourne, VIC 3207, Australia

314–321, 3rd Floor, Plot 3, Splendor Forum, Jasola District Centre, New Delhi – 110025, India

103 Penang Road, #05–06/07, Visioncrest Commercial, Singapore 238467

Cambridge University Press is part of Cambridge University Press & Assessment, a department of the University of Cambridge.

We share the University's mission to contribute to society through the pursuit of education, learning and research at the highest international levels of excellence.

www.cambridge.org
Information on this title: www.cambridge.org/9781009365499

DOI: 10.1017/9781009365482

© Dana Sawyer and Cynthia Humes 2023

This publication is in copyright. Subject to statutory exception and to the provisions of relevant collective licensing agreements, no reproduction of any part may take place without the written permission of Cambridge University Press & Assessment.

First published 2023

A catalogue record for this publication is available from the British Library.

ISBN 978-1-009-36549-9 Paperback
ISSN 2635-232X (online)
ISSN 2635-2311 (print)

Cambridge University Press & Assessment has no responsibility for the persistence or accuracy of URLs for external or third-party internet websites referred to in this publication and does not guarantee that any content on such websites is, or will remain, accurate or appropriate.

The Transcendental Meditation Movement

Elements in New Religious Movements

DOI: 10.1017/9781009365482
First published online: January 2023

Dana Sawyer
Maine College of Art

Cynthia Humes
Claremont McKenna College

Author for correspondence: Dana Sawyer (dsawyer@meca.edu).

Abstract: This Element provides a comprehensive overview of the Transcendental Meditation (TM) movement and its offshoots. Several early assessments of the TM movement as a cult and/or new religious movement are helpful, but are brief and somewhat dated. This Element examines the TM movement's history, beginning in India in 1955, and ends with an analysis of the splinter groups that have come along in the past twenty-five years. Close consideration is given to the movement's appeal for the youth culture of the 1960s, which accounted for its initial success. The Element also looks at the marketing of the meditation technique as a scientifically endorsed practice in the 1970s, and the movement's dramatic turn inward during the 1980s. It concludes by discussing the waning of its popular appeal in the new millennium. This Element describes the social and cultural forces that helped shape the TM movement's trajectory over the decades leading to the present and shows how the most popular meditation movement in America distilled into an obscure form of Neo-Hinduism.

Keywords: meditation, Maharishi, Beatles, Neo-Hinduism, gurus, New Age, Ayur Veda, Deepak Chopra, Sri Sri Ravi Shankar

© Dana Sawyer and Cynthia Humes 2023

ISBNs: 9781009365499 (PB), 9781009365482 (OC)
ISSNs: 2635-232X (online), 2635-2311 (print)

Contents

Introduction

Though there is no consensus regarding a definition of the term new religious movement or an agreed upon set of essential characteristics for the New Religious Movement (NRM) category, if we survey the various analyses of the topic for the last forty years, we find that the Transcendental Meditation (TM) movement most certainly fits inside the discussion. It is decidedly new, having reached its apex in the mid-1970s, and it is also religious, despite its claims to the contrary. Furthermore, as a religion, it is specifically best categorized as a form of Neo-Hinduism in the tradition of Shankara's Advaita Vedanta, and consequently co-relative with such movements as the Vedanta Society and the Self-Realization Fellowship. Like these, it was exported to the West by a Hindu guru, rather than imported by someone from the West.

While describing the development of the TM movement, various analyses of its similarities and differences from other and related NRMs will be shared, as will analyses developed by the academic study of NRMs. Regarding the latter, a continuous theme and thesis here is that the TM movement, as a broad category, contains two populations of supporters: an insider group of committed believers, who not only practice TM but have also accepted Maharishi Mahesh Yogi's philosophy and mission, and the far larger outsider group of casual meditators who learned TM, and may continue to practice it today, but do so on their own, with no commitment to the formal TM organization or Maharishi's Vedic Science. Understanding this division in the demographics of the movement is critical for answering the question: Is TM a religious practice? As we'll see, it most certainly is for the former group and yet not for the second group (a reality the official organization often plays upon to support its claim of being nonreligious). And this separation has numerous repercussions relative to how the TM movement can be described in connection to theories of NRMs.

Speaking in broadly descriptive terms, the TM movement fits easily within two of the eight family groups of NRMs described by J. Gordon Melton (Melton cited in Dawson 2003: 33): Family 5 of the "ancient wisdom family," in that TM is said to derive from the "immemorial" Vedic wisdom of India, and Family 7 of the "Eastern and Middle Eastern family," for the same reason. Note that it also fits within two of Lorne L. Dawson's broad categories, specifically groups associated with Asian traditions and those of the human potential movement (Dawson 1998: 14). Moreover, the TM movement carries such general characteristics of NRMs as that it was begun by a charismatic leader (a key consideration for Eileen Barker 1985); individuals joined it voluntarily; and it offered rewards beyond those of either the traditional faiths of the West or the secular establishment.

If we move our focus from the general to the particular, we still find that the TM movement has a place among NRMs, though at this level of analysis the aforementioned divisions necessarily alter the descriptors. For example, many NRMs sprang up as what the sociologist Robert Bellah has described as successor movements to those of political protest and cultural experimentation in the 1960s, and this was definitely the case for TM insiders, the majority of whom learned TM while college-aged and involved with various aspects of the counterculture. But, it should be noted that the vast majority of those who learned and may still practice TM were not drawn from this group. They *were* and *are* members of the TM movement broadly speaking, but their cultural affiliations remained with the mainstream, and what attracted them to TM dealt more with daily concerns of health and wellness than spirituality or utopianism. Consequently, if we employ a typology of NRMs like Dawson's, based on his one-variable model drawn from Max Weber, which focuses on the "mode of membership" and the "consequent form of [the NRM's] social organization" (Dawson 1998: 35), we find the TM movement is bifurcated into two groups dependent upon their degree of engagement and commitment to the formal organization. Seeking descriptive accuracy, we find useful the categories of William Sims Bainbridge and Rodney Stark (2003: 64), who propose that based on who joins and/or belongs to such groups, three types of NRMs can be identified: audience cults, client cults, and cult movements. The vast majority of TMers fall into the first two of these categories, having joined the movement either in the *audience* of people who simply purchased TM as a product or – with only a bit more commitment – developed a loose *client–consultant* relationship with their local TM center. But in contrast, TM insiders, mostly drawn from the youth culture of the 1960s and early 1970s, deeply embraced Maharishi's teachings, finding meaning and purpose in his Advaita Vedanta philosophy while also enjoying the social rewards of participating in his organization. Consequently, these insiders fall into the last of Bainbridge and Stark's categories, that is, *cult movement.*

Understanding the division between TM insiders and the casual class also influences where we position the TM movement relative to other key descriptions of NRMs. For instance, Roy Wallis (1984, 2003) has offered a tripartite typology of NRMs dependent upon their attitude toward the culture and society in which they emerge. Some NRMs are "affirming" of the values and norms of their host cultures and societies; some are "accommodating," exhibiting only mild dissatisfaction with them; and others are "rejecting" of the views and values of the world around them, sometimes even separating from it. Utilizing these yardsticks, TMers of the *audience cult* and *client cult* varieties, who today may number over 200,000, form a subclass of the *affirming* type, while TM insiders of the *cult movement* variety, hoping to generate an Age of Enlightenment with new norms and values, are members of the *accommodating* subclass and number at most a few thousand. In summary, and as we'll see more clearly later, understanding the specific views and commitments of these two subclasses is critical for understanding the TM movement as a new religious movement.

This Element begins in the 1950s, with the circumstances of Maharishi's establishment of the Spiritual Regeneration Movement (SRM), designed to enlighten all humanity. Sections 2 and 3 deal with Maharishi's realization that to accomplish this mission he must recruit and train a large number of teachers, which, by good fortune on his part, he accomplishes by appealing to the youth culture of the 1960s. Sections 4 and 5 cover Maharishi's attempt in the 1970s to distance himself from both spirituality and the counterculture by favoring scientific terminology, emphasizing the health benefits of meditation, and having his followers dress in conservative clothing. Section 5 ends with a discussion of the pivotal court case in New Jersey, in 1976, that identified TM as a religious practice, bringing the movement's heyday to a close. Maharishi's decision to turn his movement inward by asking his followers to move to Fairfield, Iowa, in 1979, along with his development of the TM-Sidhis Program, his first of several ancillary practices to TM, is dealt with in Section 6. Moving into the 1980s and early 1990s, we will discuss splinter groups that broke away from Maharishi, including those of Sri Sri Ravi Shankar and Deepak Chopra. The reactions to those apostates by the official TM organization are described in Sections 7 and 8. During the 1990s, Maharishi developed a line of health treatments and medicines based on traditional Indian medicine and collectively labeled them Maharishi Ayur Veda, and Sections 8 and 9 focus on reactions to these new programs from both within and outside Maharishi's organization. Section 10 describes the TM movement as it is today, while also offering analyses of the TM movement in relation to other new religious movements and Neo-Hindu groups.

The authors of this Element, Dana Sawyer and Cynthia Humes, met in 1984 as graduate students in the School of Religion at the University of Iowa, and have carried on a discussion about the TM movement ever since. Sawyer was a member of the TM organization from 1971 to 1983; his understanding of Maharishi's philosophy began during his six months of training in France and Switzerland (1974–5) to become a TM teacher. During that time, and while on additional advanced courses, ending in 1983, Sawyer compiled hundreds of pages of notes taken from Maharishi's lectures (delivered either in person or via videotape), establishing not only a deep understanding of Maharishi's worldview but also an insider's grasp of his organization's operation.

In addition to personal experience with Maharishi and his organization, Sawyer and Humes, who also learned TM, relied for their analyses on extensive published work (in print and online) by and about the TM movement, while also conducting dozens of interviews with TMers, beginning in 1996 and continuing until 2021. In addition, the authors engaged in extensive email and phone correspondence on specific issues – often with key figures of the movement's history, including Jerry and Debbie Jarvis, Charlie Donahue, Nancy Cooke de Herrera, Gemma Cowhig, Shannon Dickson, Robert McCutchan, Chuck Shipman, Larry Domash, Rick Archer, and John Knapp. Many sources asked that their views be shared anonymously, given either that such comments would irritate close friends or family who remain inside the group or would draw recriminations to themselves if they have remained inside. The authors request that readers understand this call for anonymity – noting that many respondents did not request it and are identified – while also pointing out that he or she can consult the acknowledgments section at the end of this Element for a longer list of primary interviewees and respondents.

1 The Very Beginning of TM

No American sect of an Asian religion or branch of what is commonly called the New Age has ever been as successful as the TM movement. During its heyday, the decade between 1968 and 1978, more than two million Americans learned to practice TM and there were TM centers in every major city of the United States and Europe. Maharishi Mahesh Yogi (1917–2008), the group's longhaired founder, became the first Indian holy man to appear on the cover of *Time* magazine since Mahatma Gandhi, and appeared as a guest for every talk show host, from Edwin Newman to Johnny Carson. A battalion of movie stars (Mia Farrow, Clint Eastwood), rock stars (the Beatles, the Rolling Stones, the Doors), professional athletes (Joe Namath, Johnny Bench), and other celebrities endorsed Maharishi's brand of meditation. Consequently, "What's your mantra?" became a common a question at cocktail parties and TM was a household word. Furthermore, even after its heyday, and even after the death of Maharishi in 2008, the TM organization (TMO) has continued to grow, and the group reports that more than six million people have been trained, today mainly with the help of the David Lynch Foundation.

Why was TM once so popular? Why did its popularity wane? What became of the TMO after its heyday? How is the TM movement similar to and different from other NRMs? How, in particular, is it similar to and different from other Neo-Hindu groups – most of which arose during the 1960s and include the followers of Sri Rajneesh, Swami Satchidananda, Yogi Bhajan, Swami Muktananda, Amrit

Desai, Sri Chinmoy, Guru Maharaji, and the Hare Krishnas (ISKCON). These are the primary questions we'll explore, unfolding the trends of thought that made the TM movement what it was – and what it became. The overall goal is to give an accurate and measured description of the group's history and significance, while also revealing points of resonance and dissonance with other NRMs. In all regards, the primary focus is on accurate description and assessment, with weighted attention to the TM movement's presence in America, given that the United States is where it has had its greatest success.

Jan Nattier has argued that various forms of Buddhism arrived in America via one of three routes: as imports brought home by Americans who embraced the religion; as exports delivered to the West by evangelical teachers from Asia; and as cultural baggage brought, figuratively speaking, to the United States in the handbags of Asian immigrants (Nattier 1997: 72). In general, Nattier's catego-ries apply equally well to American Hindu and Neo-Hindu groups, with the TM movement specifically an instance of the second type, taking root in America (and elsewhere) via the conscious efforts of its charismatic founder, Maharishi Mahesh Yogi (hereafter Maharishi). Later, most Americans would learn TM from other Americans, so there would be an import aspect to the group's profile. But in the beginning it all depended on a young monk from India.

The TM movement had its soft opening in October of 1955, when Mahesh Prasad Varma, only thirty-eight years old, and not yet titled "Maharishi," appeared in Cochin (now Kochi) at what was advertised as "The Great Spiritual Development Conference of Kerala." A souvenir booklet for Varma's talk, printed by supporters, informed attendees that he represented the "Beacon Light of the Himalayas," and would announce "The Dawn of a Happy New Era," brought to the world through "simple & easy methods of Spiritual Sadhana" (Mason 2014: 34). Touted as a spiritual luminary and "Great Seer" (i.e., *maharshi*, later anglicized as "Maharishi"), Varma's impact was entirely modest, and the growth of his movement would be slow during its first two years, hampered by the fact he was delivering a message the audience had heard innumerable times, and would hear again from other speakers at the same conference. Varma was a *brahmacari*, a student monk, in the monastic lineage of Shankara, the well-known ninth-century philosopher of Advaita Vedanta, but this gave Varma little cachet with his countrymen; he wasn't offering a new perspective, as his remarks made clear. "Remember," he told the audience that day, "it is the same age-old voice of eternal peace and happiness which the child of Kerala, the pride of India, Shri Shankara, gave out to the world more than two thousand years ago" (Mason 2014: 34).

However, the fact that his message was stale was remedied two years later, in 1957, when "Maharishi Mahesh Yogi" found a fresh audience in the West.

While appearing in Madras at another religious festival, he announced to a receptive crowd his bold plan to bring the wisdom of the Vedic Tradition to the entire world. Later he would confess he hadn't planned to initiate such a global project, soon to be called the SRM, but the crowd's enthusiasm had inspired him to do so. Consequently, he is reputed by the TMO to have rolled up his few belongings in a carpet and begun his first world tour. Within a year, he had taught his Transcendental Deep Meditation, as he labeled it in the early years, to a few hundred people and had established small meditation centers in Burma, Kuala Lumpur, Penang, Singapore, Hong Kong, and Hawaii. After Honolulu he headed to the American mainland, arriving in San Francisco on January 29, 1959, but soon moved to Los Angeles, where he established a successful base of operations (Forem 1973: 209).

In LA, Maharishi, surrounded for the first time by mostly white faces, learned quickly what appealed – and didn't appeal – to an American audience, and these lessons formed the foundation for the TM group's first talking points. In line with what Nattier described as originally appealing to American Buddhists of the import type, these first American TMers, largely middle-aged adults of the upper-middle class, placed a premium on such characteristic American values as "individualism, freedom of choice, and personal fulfillment" (Humes 2005: 57). They knew Maharishi was a Hindu monk offering the ancient wisdom of Vedic culture, but they took him at his word when he said that anyone, regardless of their religious views, could practice his meditation without compromising their own views. Furthermore, he assured them he had no plans to become their guru. Each person would simply meditate and then, as they rose further into self-realization, follow the path of their own progress – however they conceived of it – but with the assurance that expanded consciousness would lead them in the right direction. There was no required dogma, no organization to join, and no need for a personal guru. The organization he had started existed only to teach meditation, not to dictate a worldview. In summary, Maharishi learned quickly what attracted those who today fall into the demographic of "spiritual but not religious" and, as we will argue, helped establish it. Moreover, members of his first Western audience were well educated and scientifically minded; consequently, it helped that Maharishi had studied physics at Allahabad University.

What was the nature of Maharishi's meditation practice and how had he learned it? And related to these points, what philosophy was he espousing as the rational foundation for his meditation practice? Dealing with the first question, Maharishi was vague about how he had learned the procedure, usually only remarking that he was passing along the blessings of his master, Swami Brahmananda Saraswati (1871–1953), with whom Maharishi had studied for thirteen years and whom he referred to as Guru Dev, "Divine Teacher." Over the years, several conflicting assumptions arose in the TM camp, including: first, that Maharishi had been taught the technique by Brahmananda, who had corrected an ancient form of meditation that had become corrupted over time; second, that Maharishi had invented the technique himself but was given Brahmananda's blessing to do so; and third, that Maharishi and Brahmananda were both simply passing along the established technique of their monastic lineage. Today, the latter theory is most plausible, but whatever the case, the TM technique has remained consistent over the decades, involving twenty minutes of mentally repeating a mantra twice each day in the morning and evening – a practice that led Maharishi's students to coin the adage, "TM in the AM and PM."

Maharishi gave out mantras at the end of a ceremony he called puja, varieties of which are daily occurrences in pious Hindu households. A candle burned in front of a portrait of Guru Dev as Maharishi stood before it, waving incense and making offerings of water, parched rice, sandalwood paste, fruit and flowers, all the while chanting phrases in Sanskrit that sometimes included the names of Hindu gods. Then Maharishi gave the new meditator a mantra (in those days based on their gender, but later based on age), and the initiation was complete. The new initiate then performed a short meditation, and once Maharishi was certain they had practiced correctly, they were free to go home and meditate on their own ever after – with no requirement that they attend further meetings. The entire process took about an hour. But why should such an apparently simple and easy meditation practice be worth bothering with? What did these first meditators hope to gain?

Maharishi explained during his seven lectures leading up to initiation that people commonly suffer because they don't know who they are. They know themselves as a certain person with a particular gender, personality, and occupation, but they have no idea who they *really* are. Each person, he related, is a composite of two selves: a physical self made up of their mind and body, and a spiritual self that transcends their physical being. While the physical or "relative self," as Maharishi referred to it, focuses its attention on the concerns of life, such as working and raising a family, the "Absolute Self," existing at a deeper level of their being, generally goes unnoticed – though it, Maharishi contended, is the foundation of who they are. The problem is that without the experience of the Absolute Self, people lack perspective on what their life is truly about.

Maharishi explained that people vainly look outside themselves for a happiness and illumination that lies silently within everyone residing in the deeper, or higher Self. He maintained that human desire is potentially infinite, but all things that can be possessed in the physical world are finite – that is, limited by time and space. Doing the math, Maharishi argued that our *infinite* capacity for desiring can never be quenched by owning a series of *finite* objects, no matter how expensive or attractive they might be. Consequently, most people chase after happiness like duped mules, plodding endlessly after a carrot that remains ever out of reach. But – and Maharishi was effusive on this point – if we attain the experience of our absolute Self, we will own the very abode of bliss and fulfillment. Due to its infinite nature, this Self is the only gift that truly keeps on giving. To enjoy *infinitely*, we must experience *infinity*. This was Maharishi's core message. But how could this deepest level of self be realized?

Information about the Self, he related, is ultimately useless without the direct experience of it. The highest truth is not simply a body of information, but rather a direct, inner, mystical experience of the Self, and when that experience becomes permanent – an inevitable consequence of repeated contact with the Self through meditation – the meditator reaches a state of spiritual enlightenment that Maharishi referred to as Cosmic Consciousness, borrowing a term from Maurice Bucke's well-known book of that same title (1901). A person might have a clear philosophical understanding of the Self, but theories and notions are as different from it as a cake recipe is from a cake, Maharishi told his audience. The highest truth is the direct experience of the transcendent and absolute Self, hence "Transcendental Meditation."

Thus far the message may have sounded selfish to some in Maharishi's first American audience, or at least overly self-focused. It seemed to advocate that a person turn away from the world to meditate, and then, after they had reached enlightenment, to sit smugly within their own bubble of bliss. But Maharishi argued that Cosmic Consciousness – and the inner peace one would feel along the way to reaching it – would not only bring happiness to the individual, but *through* the individual to the entire world. He argued that peace grows in a society through the peace of the individuals who make it up, so if his listeners wanted world peace, they should first find inner peace. "A forest is only as green as the individual trees in the forest are green," Maharishi explained, adding that as more individuals began to meditate, more "trees in the forest" would become "green," eventually resulting in the fully green forest of an enlightened society.[1] This was the utopian aspect of Maharishi's message at that time, an aspect that would be expanded upon and augmented in the years ahead.

Maharishi giggled as he delivered his talks, and his demeanor and charisma made him an excellent advocate for his views. Seated before his students in his

---

[1] These and other quotes from Maharishi are taken directly from course notes and lectures with the guru himself, and will be recognized by TM teachers.

white robes and flowing beard, he seemed the embodiment of an enlightened sage and, perhaps best of all, he said that anyone could reach the enlightened state of consciousness – the equivalent of being a living Buddha – simply by meditating twice each day. But how, the students wondered, did the technique generate the experience of the deeper Self?

Maharishi explained that his practice was not only easy but also unique, utilizing what he termed the "natural tendency of the mind" (Mahesh Yogi 1963: 49). The mind, he observed, wanders all over the place but never does so aimlessly. The mind might seem to flit here and there without purpose, but actually it always gravitates toward that which offers it "something more." For instance, it may enjoy reading books but if the books are boring, it will effortlessly drift toward something more attractive. The mind is restless, constantly seeking out what will fulfill it most, but too often settling for temporary pleasures that distract it and ultimately leave a hangover of frustration. In reality, Maharishi contended, it actually wants to experience the boundless root of its own being. That is what the mind is always truly seeking; it wants to know the infinite level of its Self in order to enjoy itself infinitely – all as part of a process of realizing who and what it really is. Furthermore, this restless urge for more, this natural tendency of mind that occurs spontaneously, can be harnessed to allow the mind to travel inward without effort.

Maharishi told his initiates that during meditation, after sitting easily with their eyes closed for half a minute, they should begin thinking their new mantra easily, without concentrating on it. Thinking the mantra easily, he maintained, would cause the mind to stop fixating on outer objects and inner thoughts, becoming free to drift wherever it wished, and when it was completely free, it would drift inward toward its source. No mental object, he explained, is so attractive to the mind as the "source of thought" in the infinite Self. Consequently, by repeating the mantra, the mind, using its "natural tendency," would drift toward what offers it more – gravitating toward that which offers it *most*, the deep Self. As he often reiterated, "when the mind goes in the direction of the absolute bliss of the transcendent Being, it finds increasing charm at every step of its march. The mind is charmed and is led to the experience of the transcendental Being" (Mahesh Yogi 1963: 49). One only need repeat the mantra over and over effortlessly, creating a sort of drone, letting the mind float where it willed. But what if one unintentionally stopped thinking the mantra during meditation? No problem. Maharishi's instruction was simply to come back to the mantra as soon as one realized it was gone.

This is TM in a nutshell. However, after their initiation, many of Maharishi's new students were eager to learn more. As a result, Maharishi expanded upon his philosophical position during the advanced lectures open to initiates (TM meditators) only. During these talks, he elaborated on his views about the transcendental Self, explaining that it was even grander in nature than he had first let on. He explained that in the same way that we have a transcendental level of our being, so does the universe. Below the surface fluctuations of the cosmos, all of which are bound by time and space, there exists an infinite field of consciousness and energy from which all creation arises. In later TM terminology, this ground of all being is termed the field of Pure Creative Intelligence, but in the early days Maharishi referred to it as Absolute Being or simply Being, positing it as analogous to the ocean from which all waves of creation arise. The waves constitute a multiplicity, but they arise from a singularity and, in fact, they cannot be separated from the ocean. They are part of the ocean's Oneness. There is no impermeable firewall between the transcendent level of *the* Absolute Being and the finite universe that surrounds us. The latter is simply the most manifest level of the former.

Then Maharishi explained the relationship between the Absolute Being and the absolute Self. Reality is a Oneness made up of manifest things that arise from their transcendent source in the Being – and since we too, on the level of our physical selves, are some of the things arising from that transcendental Being, we too are not separate from it. Moreover, given that it is the root of all being, it is the root of *our* being. That said, students came to understand that Maharishi was equating this transcendental level of the universe with what he had termed the deep Self in earlier lectures. Therefore, when a person experienced their deep Self, they would not only experience the transcendent level of *their* being, they would also experience the transcendental level of *all* being. People do not have their own private deep Selves, he explained, each separate from the other; their deep Self is *the* deep Self of all people – and of all creation, a sort of world soul analogous to what Emerson termed the Over-Soul. The benefit of this ontology, Maharishi contended, is that when a person knows their deep or absolute Self, they are in spiritual resonance with all reality because the universe, transcendent and imminent, is a Oneness that they are in tune with at the root of their being. "In enlightenment," Maharishi explained, the meditator therefore feels the "support of almighty Nature" in everything they do (Mahesh Yogi 1969: 133).

Scholars familiar with the Advaita Vedanta of Adi Shankara (d. 750) will recognize Maharishi's message as a stripped down version of that Hindu philosophical system, with its emphasis on realizing the atman (Maharishi's Absolute or transcendental Self) as not differentiated from Brahman (Maharishi's Absolute Being). In addition, it's easy to identify Maharishi's transcendental consciousness or pure consciousness (interchangeable terms he used for the state meditators experienced when in contact with the deep Self) as identical to Advaita's *turiya* or the first stage of samadhi; Cosmic Consciousness, his term for enlightenment, is synonymous with Advaita's *jivanmukti* or *nitya-samadhi*. So why the new terms?

Maharishi didn't try, at least initially, to hide the fact that his philosophy was a traditional Hindu viewpoint; he was simply using language his students could better understand. Furthermore, as part of his Advaitin viewpoint, he believed that his philosophy was that of nature itself, implicit in the fabric of the universe, and therefore the *sanatana dharma* or eternal religion of humanity. There was no need to think of it as something exclusively Hindu, although this is not to say that Maharishi wasn't proud that Shankara, a Hindu, had articulated the position. Maharishi respected his tradition, mentioning it often and rarely appearing on stage without a portrait of his guru, Swami Brahmananda Saraswati, situated behind him. Maharishi informed his students that Shankara had founded the Dasanami lineage of monks centuries earlier, appointing leaders called Shankaracarayas, Teachers of Shankara, to preside over *vidyapiths*, seats of learning, at the four cardinal points of India. Brahmananda had been the Shankaracarya of the northern seat, located at Jyotirmath, but during the winter season, Brahmananda resided mainly at his facility in Allahabad, where Maharishi first met him in 1940. Maharishi was standing on the shoulders of giants who had kept alive this precious understanding of life's true religion for generations. Maharishi's students understood why he had such love for his tradition and guru, even though he was using different terms.

Maharishi's Advaitin teachings were fresh for many of his followers but they weren't new to America or American Neo-Hinduism. He was standing on the shoulders of Brahmananda but also on the shoulders of gurus who had come to the United States earlier, with a message nearly indistinguishable from his own. In 1893, Swami Vivekananda (1863–1902), also of the Shankara tradition, delivered a landmark address at the Parliament of the World's Religions in Chicago, introducing an audience of 7,000 to the teachings of Advaita Vedanta. Soon his popularity became so great he counted the actress Sarah Bernhardt and the inventor Nikola Tesla among his followers. Other Hindu holy men followed Vivekananda in the first wave of exported Hinduism, including Swami Paramananda (1887–1940), arriving in 1906; Paramahansa Yogananda (1893–1952), arriving in 1920; and Jiddu Krishnamurti (1895–1986), arriving in 1922. All of these also enjoyed enormous success (Trout 2001), cultivating the soil for the second wave of gurus, including Maharishi, that followed. However, even the first wave of gurus in America had had the soil prepared for them to some extent. There had been Indians who, though never visiting America, nonetheless influenced its views of Hinduism. In the eighteenth and early nineteenth centuries, descriptions of Hinduism as primitive and backward by British agents of the East India Company triggered the Bengal Renaissance, a movement led by social and religious reformer Ram Mohan Roy (1772–1833), philosopher and activist Debendranath Tagore (1817–1905), and others, characterized by an Indian pushback against denigration of their religion and culture. This movement led many in Europe and America to rethink their views, especially given that these authors described their religion in terms attractive to the Western mind, claiming that Hinduism was just an alternative pathway to the same God – a viewpoint that Vivekananda specifically emphasized at the Parliament of 1893.

Furthermore, this fertile soil wasn't cultivated by Indians alone, at least not directly, for in the nineteenth century there had also been a first wave of imported Hinduism. Early translations of Hindu scriptures, including Charles Wilkins' translation of the Bhagavad Gita (1785), generated an enormous influence on European philosophy, registering notably in the work of German philosophers Friedrich Schlegel (1772–1829), Arthur Schopenhauer (1788–1860), and Friedrich Schelling (1775–1854). Through a meeting with Samuel Taylor Coleridge (1772–1834), Ralph Waldo Emerson (1803–82) was introduced to the work of Schelling, a friend of Coleridge, and as a result, many of Schelling's Indian-influenced ideas helped shape New England Transcendentalism. Emerson's extraordinary popularity during the last decades of the nineteenth century did much to prepare the way for the first wave of gurus, including Vivekananda, who arrived in America just five years after Emerson's death.

Maharishi's students enjoyed a resource not available to Emerson, however, having a living Hindu monk willing to share the actual technique for reaching enlightenment. In Maharishi they found not only a vision but also a way. And so Maharishi gathered around him, in 1959, a small but devoted inner circle of students, including Arthur and Chris Granville, Charlie and Helen Lutes, David and Jessamine Verrill, Helena and Roland Olson, and John Hislop. This inner circle was the first iteration of the TMO in the West, but there was a hitch in their plan to spiritually regenerate the world. Even if Americans caught on to Maharishi's message, there was only so much time for him to teach. Consequently, Maharishi decided to multiply himself by training teachers, announcing a new project in the fall of 1959, in Sequoia National Park, at the first international meeting of the SRM. Charlie Lutes later explained the rational, observing, "if the guru could not be everywhere at once, his cadre of initiators could be everywhere for him" (Lutes 1968: 5).

2 Maharishi Multiplies Himself

Maharishi's movement was growing, and would soon expand exponentially. Over the next twenty years, Maharishi would train more than 10,000 teachers, and they would in turn teach more than two million people in the United States alone, a number equal to four times the present population of Wyoming. But in

1960, Maharishi had to first find people interested in becoming TM teachers. Some from the Los Angeles group were eager, but Maharishi needed teachers in other cities as well – and in other countries – and these people would first have to discover that Maharishi existed. To that end, he resumed his world tour soon after the meeting in Sequoia.

Arriving in London in 1960, Maharishi settled briefly into a modest apartment in the Knightsbridge section of town, and this occasioned an important episode in the formation of his movement. One night early in his visit, he was asked to speak at the London School of Economics (LSE) to a group that followed the esoteric teachings of G. I. Gurdjieff (d. 1949) and P. D. Ouspensky (1878–1947), Gurdjieff's Russian disciple. Maharishi accepted the offer and was quickly welcomed and celebrated by the group as an anticipated savior (Maynard 1968: 129). Ouspensky had broken with Gurdjieff in Paris in 1924, but went on to become the major proponent of Gurdjieff's ideas. In 1928, Ouspensky reported that his true purpose was to organize a serious-minded group that would attract the attention of a great teacher from the East, which would complete Gurdjieff's mission on earth. This teaching of Ouspensky predisposed the London group to keep an eye out for gurus who fit their messianic expectations. In the 1950s, an Indonesian spiritual teacher named Pak Subuh (1901–87), touting a system he called Subud, had appealed to some members of the group, but only a few had broken away to follow him. Now it was Maharishi's turn to be embraced by those who remained, and they eagerly did so.

Maharishi was initially pleased with the warm welcome and happy to be the predicted prophet. The group quickly spread Maharishi's message to other followers of Gurdjieff in England, and the next year, during Maharishi's second visit to London, they even managed to arrange for him to speak at Royal Albert Hall, on May 13, 1961. The success of this event stirred so much interest in Maharishi that the group opened a School of Meditation, with Maharishi delivering an inspiring inaugural address, explaining that they would awaken the world through TM. But to his consternation, the project quickly imploded. The problem was that the group that met at LSE could not be weaned off their devotion to Gurdjieff and Ouspensky, seeing Maharishi's system of meditation as only an addendum, however important, to the teachings of their previous masters. As a consequence, rather than pulling the London group into his way of thinking, Maharishi found himself appropriated into theirs. Reaching an impasse, he soon left London, causing the group to lose faith in him. But they didn't lose faith in TM, which they continued to practice and teach on their own – without Maharishi's oversight or blessing (Maynard 1968: 125–29). This appropriation of TM by the Ouspensky-ites seems foundational for creating Maharishi's obsession ever after with keeping the teaching pure.

Maharishi decided he had to be more protective of his teachings, and more careful of how he presented them, or he would lose control of what he had brought from India. Specifically, he reasoned it would be best to formalize his teachings into an exclusive brand that could not be simply added to the teachings of others. To accomplish this, he increasingly standardized his teachings over the next two years, codifying them in his first book, *The Science of Being and Art of Living* (1963), while also working toward trademarking his TM practice. Furthermore, to insure that the branches of the SRM he was leaving behind didn't stray from the correct interpretation of his teachings, he mailed audiotapes of his lectures back to them from his tours. This practice also worked well for keeping up interest, and between 1961 and 1965, it was Maharishi's primary method of staying in touch with his followers – with SRM centers now in the United States, Canada, England, Germany, Sweden, India, Burma, Ceylon, and Australia. After the Gurdjieff affair, Maharishi also decided to insure quality control of his teachings by formulating a strict program of instruction for his new cadre of TM teachers. If these teachers could be trained not to deviate from his views – based on his repeated assertion that it would corrupt the purity of the teaching and offend the holy tradition of saints who had passed it down to him – he would be multiplying himself in a way that did not threaten his control of his message. Furthermore, it would inaugurate a standardized brand that offered exactly the same message, no matter where it was encountered, while also, slowly but surely, initiating the rigid structures of the later TMO.

In early 1961, SRM groups from all over the world learned that Maharishi's first teacher training course (TTC) would be held in the Himalayas, supposedly to give his teachers more prestige with the public than if he held the course in the United States or Europe (Dragemark 1972: 43). Subsequently, a thirteen-acre site was secured on the banks of the Ganges at Rishikesh, a Hindu pilgrimage center, and a small complex was erected and dedicated as the Dhyan Vidya Peeth ("the Seat of Meditation Knowledge"). After three months of attending Maharishi's lectures, meditating for eight to ten hours per day, and doing little else, the group was informed by the guru that sixteen of the thirty-five were eligible to be teachers. This group was taken aside and given the two mantras they would thereafter bestow during initiations, with one mantra for men and one for women. This number would increase over the years – to eight mantras in 1969, nine in 1972, and sixteen in 1976. Beulah Smith, a middle-aged woman from San Diego, California, became the first American TM teacher, and would remain the only one until 1966.

Resuming his world travels, while stopping in Los Angeles, Maharishi took notice of a promising young member of the SRM group named Jerry Jarvis.

He and his wife Debby had learned TM during Maharishi's previous visit, and soon Jerry would rise to become the closest thing to a second-in-command Maharishi would ever allow – Charlie Lutes (and later, Deepak Chopra) notwithstanding. Jerry and Debby, full of enthusiasm, were former newspaper reporters and half a generation younger than most members of the inside group. Jerry was also an articulate speaker with a peaceful demeanor and compelling personality. Consequently, Maharishi began grooming Jerry to become an initiator. The first step in that process began in November of 1961, during a three-week retreat on Catalina, an island on the California coast near Los Angeles. Both Jerry and Debby attended and were trained with twenty others to give the seven scripted lectures that led up to initiation. In addition, the attendees learned how to check a meditator's use of the mantra to insure correct meditation. In the near future, this lower tier of TM functionaries would be called checkers, and Jon Michael Miller provides a good description of their function in his book *A Wave in the Ocean* (Miller 2006: 159). Following the course, Jarvis proved immediately to be inspiring, so much so that he was chosen to travel all over California giving lectures, with Beulah Smith following after him to perform initiations. In 1966, he would become an initiator himself, in fact the most successful initiator of all time, personally initiating more than 5,000 people, while lecturing to thousands more.

In 1962, Maharishi hosted a second retreat on Catalina and was introduced to Nancy Cooke de Herrera, a forty-year-old socialite and cultural ambassador to Argentina, who passionately embraced his mission and worked to get Maharishi in with high society (Cooke de Herrera 1992). Nancy, an heiress to the bobby pin fortune, introduced Maharishi to the tobacco heiress Doris Duke, who immediately donated 100,000 dollars to improve the guru's ashram in India, upgrading it to the form the Beatles enjoyed during their visit five years later. Maharishi's message was getting out, but the pace continued to be glacial. In 1965, after six years of concerted effort, there were barely more than 200 meditators in the entire United States. Nancy had helped boost Maharishi's financial resources, and she would later teach TM to several high-profile celebrities, including Greta Garbo, Madonna, and Cheryl Crow, but for the moment initiations were rare. Suddenly Maharishi's luck changed.

In the early 1960s, the guru had devoted more of his time to Europe than America, finding greater success there, but in 1966 Jerry Jarvis discovered a new audience. Jarvis recalled during an interview that a young man from El Camino College in Manhattan Beach asked him to give a lecture to twenty or thirty of his friends, and the friends became so eager to learn TM that Jarvis completed the seven required lectures in only two nights – setting a precedent for the two-lecture format used ever after in the TMO (Forem 1973: 215; Ebon 1975: 81). Realizing he was onto something, while noting that the volume of applicants demanded he not be dependent on Beulah Smith for initiations, Jarvis attended that spring's TTC. Returning to California from India, Jerry and Debbie, also now a teacher, immediately began increasing the momentum of Maharishi's movement, initiating students at UCLA, Stanford, and other universities. In *American Veda*, Philip Goldberg reports: "At the end of 1965 only 220 Americans had learned TM. When 1968 began, there were nearly 5,000, and by the election of Richard Nixon that November, the number had tripled" (Goldberg 2010: 162). This expansion was the direct result of Jarvis' new focus on college students, and soon he formed a subsidiary of the SRM called the Students International Meditation Society (SIMS), specifically designed to capture the youth culture's enthusiasm.

Less than two years after the formation of SIMS, the Beatles – and The Doors, the Grateful Dead, and other rock groups – would give a tremendous boost to Maharishi's mission, but it is important to note that even before the Beatles and others' involvement something powerful had been happening with the youth culture. In fact, the Beatles were drawn to Maharishi for the same reasons as others of their generation. This is significant in that it helps explain why even after the Beatles separated from Maharishi (more on this later) his movement kept growing. In 1966, due to the baby boom phenomenon, nearly half of the population of the United States was under twenty-five, and this new generation – less invested in the traditional religions of their parents, and more open to ideas focused on self-improvement – was eager to meditate. In the years ahead, this youth culture would be characterized variously as a return to romanticism (Paglia 1990), a renewed search for meaning (Bellah et al. 1985), and so on, but in all cases the emerging counterculture was driven by the same set of influences. Sociologist of religion Lorne L. Dawson has accurately summarized these influences as "the civil rights movement, the student power movement, the feminist movement, the war against poverty, the ecological movement, and most important, the often violent protest against the war in Vietnam, and the military draft" (Dawson 1998: 44).

Like the Beat Generation before it, the youth culture created a spontaneous and informal academy of its own. As Charles Perry has explained in his book *The Haight-Ashbury*: "It was almost as if an international youth movement were holding a symposium where ideas were taken up, passed around and commented on with great rapidity, all beyond the comprehension of the world's grown-ups" (Perry 1984: 53). This culture was beginning to burgeon on college campuses in 1966, and Maharishi, via Jerry Jarvis, was poised to take advantage of it. He had found a new doorway into the American psyche – or, more accurately, it had found him. Over the next three years, hundreds of young people would line up at their local TM centers in the hopes of augmenting or replacing their current mottos of "Do your own thing," "Hell no, we won't go," and "Don't trust anybody over thirty" with Sanskrit mantras that would make them living Buddhas.

Maharishi's popularity grew so quickly that the mainstream media took notice. On December 17, 1967, the *New York Times* Sunday magazine proclaimed Maharishi the "Chief Guru of the Western World" (Goldberg 2010: 157), prompting the TMO to schedule two appearances for him at elite venues on the East Coast. The first event, held on Sunday, January 21, 1968, attracted a sold-out audience of more than 3,000 to the Felt Forum of New York City's Madison Square Garden. The second packed Harvard's Sanders Hall, with the actress Mia Farrow sitting prominently in the front row. These events were immediately followed by appearances on *The Tonight Show* and the *Today Show* and abruptly Maharishi was a household name. This boost in publicity triggered an increased demand for TM, which in turn triggered a need for TM initiators. Luckily, this trend had already been anticipated. When Maharishi wrapped up his public appearances in New York, he flew straight to India to train new teachers, with Mia Farrow on the same flight. Both would soon be joined in India by the Beatles, Donovan, Mike Love of the Beach Boys, Nancy Cooke de Herrera, and fifty other students, the majority of whom were under thirty years old. Transcendental Meditation's heyday was about to begin.

3 Maharishi Embraces the Love Generation

Maharishi's original message had a very specific recipe: he would enlighten the world by enlightening the individuals who make it up. Likewise, his description of enlightenment, synonymous with that found in Shankara's Advaita philosophy, was also specific. Maharishi's two primary books, the aforementioned *Science of Being* (1963) and his *On the Bhagavad Gita* (first published in 1967), describe an enlightened state in which one experiences "both levels of their being," spiritual and physical, absolute and relative. By repeatedly alternating their consciousness between these two states, people cultivate over time a condition in which both levels of self are experienced simultaneously. By this process, he claimed, the eventual, and inevitable, result of regular meditation was Cosmic Consciousness.

Maharishi was also crystal clear about the benefits of achieving this elevated state. He maintained that it would bring not only inner peace but also inner bliss, and that it would remove all fear of death, given that the transcendental Self can never die. On an ethical level, another benefit, often emphasized, is that in enlightenment one need not worry about the morality of one's actions.

Maharishi asserted that having merged their individual consciousness with the source of all consciousness, the "knower of Brahman" enjoys an ethical freedom based on "spontaneous right action" (Mahesh Yogi 1969: 361–3). Whatever one does in enlightenment *must* be ethical, Maharishi argued, because their personal consciousness is in constant resonance with the source of everything. Furthermore, all actions instigated by an enlightened person must be beneficial to the cosmic purpose for the same reason. Maharishi had written that

> when the Lord [Krishna] began to instruct Arjuna in the art of spontaneous right action [he] advised him to come out of the field of relativity and take his stand in the field of the Absolute; he would thereby rise to that state of life – cosmic consciousness – where one becomes capable of performing actions in complete accordance with the laws of nature, thus fulfilling one's dharma and serving the cosmic purpose. (Mahesh Yogi 1969: 192)

A common assumption among initiators, derived from this notion of spontaneous right action, was that the actions of an enlightened person which may appear to be immoral, impractical, or disadvantageous must, on closer scrutiny, prove not to be. It wasn't the place of the unenlightened to judge the cosmic purpose; they must learn to trust the vision of the awakened guru, in this case Maharishi. Consequently, as Maharishi changed his mind or formed new plans, these should be accepted as directives of the cosmic will, to be supported as additions to the holy tradition to be maintained in their purity. Looking ahead for a moment, as the TMO grew, this dynamic of strict adherence to Maharishi's wishes – even if only reported to insiders by his lieutenants – would often translate into dogmatic policies that contradicted the expectation of meditators soon becoming maharishis themselves, enjoying spontaneous right actions of their own – and therefore not needing to be told what to do. However, an important addendum here is that Maharishi seems to have rarely engaged in behavior that was off-putting or immoral (at least publicly), as, for instance, was the case with such gurus as Bubba Free John (aka Adi Da, 1939–2008) or Fredrick Lenz (1950–1998), both of whom justified their erratic behavior on the grounds that they were shaking disciples out of their non-evolutionary patterns.

Over time, Maharishi provided refinements to his initial description of enlightenment, including adding the higher states of God Consciousness, Unity Consciousness, and Brahman Consciousness. But these all depended upon Cosmic Consciousness as the entry level of enlightenment, and so it was the primary aim of his initiators and inner circle.

TMers in general wondered what it would be like to be enlightened, but they needn't look any further than Maharishi for the answer. He was the model of what they hoped to become. True, he had never actually said he was enlightened, but neither had he ever denied it. Some insiders felt frustrated that he didn't clear the air on this matter, hoping he would just come out and admit it, but he never did. William Gibson, the playwright who wrote *The Miracle Worker*, once spent time on a TM teacher training course, which he described in his book *A Season in Heaven*, 1974. He joked about Maharishi's silence on the subject, commenting that the robe-clad guru, "played his cards mighty close to his dhoti" (Gibson 1974: 175). But Maharishi's followers, urged by their higher-ups, believed that he was just extraordinarily humble. Besides, he had explained that it was not traditional for Hindu monks to talk about their state of awakening, so they contented themselves with that. Whatever the case, everyone in the organization believed unequivocally that the guru was enlightened, which is why Jack Forem, a movement spokesperson, once comfortably claimed: "In his book *Love and God* Maharishi describes the state of life of one who has risen to the highest peaks of human possibility. Because the words are written from the state of realization that they describe, they are a beautiful and precise self-portrait" (Forem 1973: 206).

However, when it came to grasping what enlightenment was like, TMers had another key reference point. A majority of Maharishi's students from the youth culture – which was *the* majority of his students – believed they had already glimpsed enlightenment during experiences with psychedelics, drugs they had proudly listed on their application forms to learn TM. In the late 1960s and 1970s, Maharishi worked hard to discourage any association between psychedelic experience and spiritual experience but there's no doubt he benefited from the connection. "Drugs," religion scholar Lola Williamson explained while discussing TM, "particularly those psychedelic drugs such as mescaline and LSD – gave young people a taste of mystical experience and a craving for more of the same" (Williamson 2010: 45). This craving led them to Maharishi, as Allen Ginsberg (1926–1997), the Beat poet and philosopher, once pointed out to the guru. Immediately following Maharishi's appearance at the Felt Forum on January 21, 1968, he was taken by limo to a VIP gathering at the Plaza Hotel. While sitting close beside the guru, Ginsberg asked what Maharishi thought of LSD, only to be told it was a waste of time. Ginsberg then reputedly infused the gathering with some spunk by remarking, "There wouldn't be all these people sitting around here listening to you if it wasn't for LSD" (Goldberg 2010: 158; see also Ebon 1975: 20).

Maharishi was nonplussed by the comment and quickly changed the subject, but the poet was certainly correct; the view that psychedelic drugs could trigger glimpses of enlightenment was endemic to the youth culture of the mid-1960s. Tracing its history briefly to provide some reference points, Aldous Huxley (1894–1963), who had studied Vedanta with Swami

Prabhavananda (1893–1976) in Los Angeles, first crafted the meme by drawing parallels between psychedelic experience and enlightened consciousness in *The Doors of Perception* (1954). Then, in 1960, Harvard psychologist Timothy Leary (1920–1996) began championing Huxley's viewpoint to anyone who would listen, and was soon joined in print by Huston Smith (1919–2016), then the renowned professor of world religions at MIT. In 1962, popular philosopher Alan Watts (1915–1973) also reinforced the Huxley meme in *The Joyous Cosmology* (1962). Four years later, in 1966, Leary, and his colleagues Richard Alpert (later called Ram Dass) and Ralph Metzner, published *The Psychedelic Experience*, a handbook for insuring safe arrival into awakened consciousness while tripping on acid. This handbook, along with books by Watts and Huxley, were on every hippie coffee table of the mid-1960s – in other words, exactly when Ginsberg met Maharishi.

Understanding this assumption of the counterculture is important to the present study because it also influenced the Beatles' decision to follow Maharishi. The four Brits, then (and still) the most popular musical group ever to perform, had embraced not only Leary's appetite for LSD but also the Advaita Vedanta interpretation of psychedelic awakening he had inherited from Huxley. Consequently, we find evidence of that connection not only in Leary's writings but also in the Beatles' music. For example, in the song "Tomorrow Never Knows" (1966), John Lennon shared lyrics he had copied directly from Leary's *The Psychedelic Experience*, endorsing the value of opening up to the Ground of Being during an acid trip: "Lay down all thoughts, surrender to the void. ... That you may see the meaning of within. It is Being. It is Being."

However, the Beatles quickly added made an addition to their specific message: psychedelics gave glimpses of the goal but meditation could turn those flashes of illumination into an abiding light. Williamson relates that the message of meditation replacing acid originated with Ram Dass (Williamson 2010: 46), who indeed reinforced it in *Be Here Now* (1971), but it actually began with Huxley, as Harrison Pope Jr., the first scholar to closely scrutinize the youth culture's embrace of Asian religions, pointed out in *The Road East* (Pope 1974: 30). The Beatles had picked up on Huxley's view and asserted it publicly soon after their first meeting with Maharishi, in August of 1967.

George Harrison was the first Beatle to become interested in Hindu culture and music, but when one Beatle became interested in something, the others soon followed. Consequently, when George's wife, Pattie Boyd, learned that Maharishi was to speak at the Park Lane Hilton in London, all four members of the group attended, on August 24, 1967. Two days later, after learning TM, the Beatles publicly renounced drugs at a press conference, claiming to have "gone beyond it" (Goldman 1988: 326). In an interview with David Frost,

Lennon explained that as far as the Beatles were concerned, acid was out and meditation was in: "[TM] is the biggest thing in our lives at the moment," Lennon commented, "and it's come at a time when we need it. We want to learn the meditation thing properly, so we can sell the whole idea to everyone" (Ebon 1975: 57). To that end, the group decided to attend Maharishi's training course in India that winter/spring of 1968. John and George were the first Beatles to arrive there, on February 16, flying in with their wives and met at the Delhi airport by Mia Farrow, who had come with her sister, Prudence – soon the subject of the song "Dear Prudence." Paul and Ringo arrived four days later, joining the sixty meditators at Maharishi's ashram (which today is a state park and tourist attraction). In just three months, Maharishi hoped to make the Beatles new teachers, but before the course ended, all members of the group had left.

Things began well and the Beatles had enjoyed their Himalayan idyll. But Maharishi's blissful relationship with them ended in crisis after only a few weeks. The popular versions of what happened touted by the press claimed that the split occurred because Maharishi had broken his monastic vows by soliciting sex from one or more of his female students. Whatever may or may not have taken place, John and George believed the charge and fled the course (Ringo and Paul had already left for personal reasons), and two months later, while promoting their new album on *The Tonight Show*, John and Paul explained that they had been mistaken about Maharishi, and that he had turned out to be "only a man." Later, John further expressed his indignation in a song originally titled "Maharishi" but later changed to "Sexy Sadie," including the lyric, "You made a fool of everyone."

After the separation from the Beatles, the press uniformly predicted the end of Maharishi's teaching career. The popular magazine *Screenplay* commented, "The Beatles began the Maharishi cult – and in all probability, the Beatles have now ended it" (Ebon 1975: xii). But the predictions were entirely off for reasons we've already discussed; specifically, it was the youth culture's interest in Maharishi's teachings – and Asian religions in general – that had led the Beatles to Maharishi in the first place. The Beatles, after all, were also members of what was labeled the love generation. Related to that fact, Ian MacDonald has pointed out, "The Beatles weren't so much causing the great social and psychological changes of that era as mirroring them" (MacDonald 2005: 31). As a result, young people kept coming, drawn to the guru's message of reaching enlightenment in spite of the Beatles. Perhaps the group had been mistaken about what happened? This is what TM insiders also accepted as the truth of the matter, on the grounds that Maharishi – whose actions are instinctively correct – could never have done something wrong. (George, Paul, and Ringo later apologized to Maharishi in person, saying they had been wrong to judge him on the basis of gossip. In April 1992, George even gave a benefit concert at Royal Albert Hall for the TMO – his last full-length concert before dying in 2001.)

The youth culture – now dubbed Woodstock Nation by the radical Yippie Abbie Hoffman (1936–1989) – provided an enormous market for gurus, whether they were from India or of the Nattier import type. Therefore, all Maharishi had to do to increase his numbers was to keep making new teachers, and there was no shortage of applicants. As an appendix to this point, recruits for Maharishi's courses self-selected to join the guru, buoyed by their own utopian enthusiasm, with no evidence they were ever coerced. Having learned TM, most of them simply wanted more of what Maharishi was offering and training courses were the place to get it. While Beulah Smith had been the sole TM initiator in the United States until 1966, according to Jack Forem (relying on the movement's records):

> [B]y 1969 the number had grown to 200; just three years later, in June of 1972, there were 2,400; and after a very successful course in the Spanish resort town of La Antilla, another 600 were added in the summer of 1973, bringing the total of United States teachers to more than 3,000 – with nearly as many others spread out over the rest of the world." (Forem 1973: 218)

Three thousand young Americans practicing TM was one thing, but 3,000 young Americans able to teach TM was something else. Maharishi had indeed multiplied himself.

By late 1975, the efforts of these young teachers would translate into hundreds of thousands of TMers in the United States alone; however, returning to 1968, and just after the breakup with the Beatles, the future didn't look so promising for one simple reason. Maharishi had become deeply identified in the Zeitgeist with the hippies of the counterculture; he even looked like a hippie with his long hair, beard, and beads, and this association made him unattractive to the mainstream. Therefore, in 1970, Maharishi began implementing plans to distance himself from the counterculture, including making a move to drop all spiritual language. But it wasn't clear he could entice his young followers to join him.

4 Discovering Inner Energy and Overcoming Stress

Maharishi had accessed a strata of intelligent Americans who had not yet established a career and were therefore free to help him save the world. In 1970, the year that Maharishi was given the "Man of Hope Award" by the United Nations, the first TTC ever held in the United States took place in the resort community of Poland Spring, Maine, with several hundred students attending in June. Later that summer, a larger crowd gathered on the campus of the California State University in Humboldt, California. While these TTCs involved a month-long introduction to Maharishi's philosophy, to become initiators students also had to attend an additional three-month course. Two of these longer courses were held that winter: one in Estes Park, Colorado, and another on the island of Majorca, Spain. These two programs yielded Maharishi more than 1,000 new teachers – nearly 800 from Majorca alone. One result of this rapidly expanding cadre of initiators was that more people learned TM in 1971 than had learned in all previous years combined. More teachers meant more meditators, and more meditators meant more students who wanted to become teachers. Though still largely out of the public's eye, the momentum of the TM movement had kicked into high gear. The following summer, more than 1,000 new students attended the month-long course at Amherst, Massachusetts, 1,000 more attended the August course at Humboldt, and the winter course, again in Majorca but later moved to Fiuggi, Italy, created more initiators than had previously existed. Then, in 1972–73, a course in La Antilla, Spain, added another thousand teachers.

Maharishi reinforced his students' hopes for an Age of Aquarius, but his connections with the youth culture alienated him from the masses, an audience he was eager to reach. But if he explicitly disparaged the youth culture – that is, the culture that had made him successful – could it slow his momentum? Between 1966 and 1970, he straddled the ideological fence, commonly labeled the generation gap, reinforcing young people's shared hopes for personal and collective awakening while simultaneously placating their parents by speaking out against drug use and revolutionary politics. However, Maharishi believed that if he truly hoped to spiritually regenerate the world, he must appeal to people over thirty. To that end, he drafted a set of new initiatives, including the charge that his followers should bathe more, cut their hair, and wear less garish clothes. He explained it was prudent to meet people at their own level in pursuit of the TM movement's greater goal. "TMers," as they often called themselves, wouldn't alter their mission; they would simply change their appearance to fulfill it more easily. In 1971, during the month-long course in Massachusetts, Maharishi told his students, "Throw your jeans into the ocean," and they did just that (or rather, put them in their closets), replacing tie-dyed t-shirts with suits and ties, trading sandals for shoes, swapping miniskirts for calf-length dresses, and putting away their love beads. All things considered, this directive proved highly successful. Parents were pleased that their adult children practicing TM had cut their hair, stopped smoking pot, and dressed more respectably. With the endorsement of parents – many of whom learned TM – other individuals over thirty also took interest.

Back in 1962, Maharishi had formed a separate organization besides the SRM to promote TM to those less spiritually inclined than his SRM followers. In 1970, the International Meditation Society (IMS), and its affiliate, the SIMS, attracted the most meditators. With Maharishi's deployment of newly clean-cut teachers, TM's appeal skyrocketed. Like many other gurus who had come to America, Maharishi had stopped talking about reincarnation and other aspects of Hinduism that were unappealing for Westerners. Charlie Lutes, director of the SRM, continued to hold forth on spiritual matters, but as Robert McCutchan, a TM insider who later became a literature professor, makes clear, Maharishi's recalibrated message was squarely focused on the psychological, physical, and social benefits of regular meditation (McCutchan 1977: 146). Thus, some of Maharishi's earlier publications, including *Love and God* (1965) and *Meditations of the Maharishi* (1968), both laden with God talk, were downplayed to the public by IMS and SIMS, hidden away in closets with initiators' torn jeans.

By early 1971, Maharishi's Advaita Vedanta message had morphed into the Science of Creative Intelligence (SCI). When speaking about the eternal, unchanging Brahman at the root of all existence, teachers were instructed to no longer use the term Absolute Being; instead, it was Pure Creative Intelligence. Spiritually loaded terms such as Divine Consciousness, used so often by Maharishi in his Bhagavad Gita commentary, were dropped, and "transcendental consciousness" or "pure consciousness" became the exclusive terms for that state of being. Years earlier, Maharishi had abandoned talk of *samskaras*, the mental impressions from past lives that dictate our present behavior, preferring to characterize them as "stress" from earlier trauma. In the 1970s, the appeal of TM as an antidote to stress gained support from several preliminary studies on meditators. For example, a questionnaire-based study by W. Thomas Winquist at UCLA in 1969 (Winquist 1976) indicated that TM was effective for drawing young people away from drugs; a different study by Demetri Kanellakos, a senior researcher at Stanford Research Institute, provided evidence that TMers had increased energy and efficiency (Kanellakos & Lukas 1974). Most significantly, a research project in physiology undertaken at UCLA revealed that the rest gained during TM was more than twice as deep as the deepest point in sleep. In 1972, this study by Robert Keith Wallace was replicated at Harvard Medical School by Wallace and Dr. Herbert Benson (Wallace & Benson 1972). Transcendental Meditation received an enormous boost when Hans Selye (1974), an expert on stress-related illness, read the article and publicly endorsed TM on the grounds that deeper rest could help eliminate stress too deeply rooted for sleep alone to remove.

The new iteration of Maharishi's philosophy – sounding secular and supported by science – resonated not only with the public but also with the medical profession. Doctors began prescribing TM for patients with stress disorders such as high blood pressure, migraine headaches, ulcers, asthma, insomnia, and a range of other maladies. With the help of physicians and psychiatrists, Maharishi began attracting luminaries of the American intelligentsia, including Buckminster Fuller, Harvey Brooks, Mael A. Melvin, and Linus Pauling. Despite Maharishi's personal appearance, his days of flower power and the Beatles were over. Transcendental Meditation was about helping people to relieve stress, perform better at work, quit smoking, and get along better at home, not self-realization or Divine Consciousness.

Martin Ebon, a long-time Maharishi observer, claimed that 1972 was the turnaround year for Maharishi's true success, specifically because scientific research supporting the health benefits of TM began appearing in such publications as *Science, Scientific American*, and the *Lancet*. As acceptance of Maharishi's reformulated message grew, the popular press jumped on the bandwagon, featuring stories on TM in *Ladies Home Journal, Redbook, Psychology Today,* and *Time*. In addition to glowing media accounts, several bestsellers penned by TM insiders quickly followed, including Jean Robbins and David Fisher's *Tranquility Without Pills* (1973), Harold Bloomfield's *TM: Discovering Inner Energy and Overcoming Stress* (1974), Denise Denniston and Peter McWilliams' *The TM Book: How to Enjoy the Rest of Your Life* (1975), and Peter Russell's *The TM Technique* (1976). This was TM's heyday and when, in 1975, Maharishi appeared on two episodes of the popular *Merv Griffin Show*, flanked on stage by such stars of television and cinema as Mary Tyler Moore and Clint Eastwood, TM centers could barely keep up with the number of people seeking initiation. Inside the TMO today, this tsunami of interest is still referred to as the Merv Wave, and the impact was enormous. The popular talk show programs aired in more than a hundred cities, giving thirty to forty million viewers what Goldberg refers to as a "Cliff Notes version of Vedanta 101" (Goldberg 2010: 166).

Not everyone was happy about Maharishi's popularity, however, or with his thinly disguised message. Some commentators described his switch to scientific terminology as a case of working the angles of a "snake oil salesman" (White 1976: 128). Some even accused him of crafting a Trojan horse, hiding his true intention of converting people to Hinduism inside a secular package of pseudo-scientific jargon. John Weldon, a conservative Christian, claimed in his book *The Transcendental Explosion* (Weldon 1976: 67) that Maharishi's SCI was only Hindu wine poured into new bottles, with its name changed to dupe the innocent. Weldon's accusations were often hyperbolic, but John White, a respected public intellectual on issues related to consciousness expansion, also recognized Maharishi's tactic, observing that "science is the religion of our society and scientists are the high priests. The aura of science is especially effective in selling something. . . . The TM Movement recognizes this clearly and uses science to sell TM" (White 1976: 85). Related to this, the vast majority of interviewees surveyed (see acknowledgments section), ranging over more than a ten-year period, and including Jerry Jarvis, supported White's claim, but found nothing wrong with the tactic. In fact, disguising TM's spiritual content with neologisms and scientific charts was, for most interviewees, a secret hiding in plain view. Charlie Lutes, the SRM leader, agreed, once explaining to Robert Bellah, then dean of American sociologists of religion, that the shift had no intent other than to make TM more accessible. "The popularization of the movement in non-spiritual terms," Lutes contended, "was strictly for the purpose of gaining the attention of the people who wouldn't have paid the movement much mind if it had been put in spiritual terms" (Lutes quoted in Dawson 2003: 54) However, neither Lutes nor the majority of individuals we interviewed believed Maharishi's new approach was a trick for converting people to Hinduism. They didn't believe it then and few of them believe it now.

Maharishi had stated clearly from the beginning that TM was not Hinduism, nor was it part of any other religion; it was a practical technology for self-realization that didn't rely on faith. In short, during the 1970s Maharishi's teachers accepted his definitions of both Hinduism and religion, though they were willing to admit, at least to each other, that their goal remained spiritual. They aimed to help the world achieve the same enlightenment they hoped for themselves, and if the new lingo helped accomplish that goal, they saw no problem. Mainstream Americans had no interest in such things, but if they learned TM and kept at it, they might eventually realize that using TM to quit smoking or perform better at work was only touching the first level of benefits. Transcendental Meditation teachers believed that simply by practicing TM, devotees would ascend spiritually and eventually realize that what they really wanted was enlightenment. Even if the teachers were a bit disingenuous about TM's Hindu roots, they would be thanked one day. It wasn't hypocrisy, it was kindness. Transcendental Meditation teachers felt no disconnect as they performed puja ceremonies that included the names of Hindu gods, repeated Sanskrit mantras, read the Bhagavad Gita, followed a vegetarian diet, listened to recordings of Sama Veda, and still believed they weren't Hindus.

The perspective of TM insiders was that SCI captured the essence of all religions and belonged to none of them exclusively; thus the question of whether the SCI, including TM, was Hinduism was moot. It was the ideology endemic to the universe itself, and would arise effortlessly in the mind of anyone who reached Cosmic Consciousness. It wasn't humanly created. It was in the Bhagavad Gita but didn't depend upon anything related to Hinduism. A clear cognition of nature's implicit truth existed in India, and especially in Shankara's teachings, but this was the only reason there was a connection to the subcontinent. Hinduism was a religion focused on caste distinctions, child marriage, prayers, rituals, and guru worship, but Maharishi put no emphasis on such practices. Individuals were in charge of their thoughts and actions, not Maharishi.

These views overlook the fact that the Bengali Renaissance of the late eighteenth to early twentieth centuries had already trimmed Hinduism down to its supposed essential core, discarding the very elements Maharishi also left out, while emphasizing nearly the same worldview. Bengali reformers had also hoped to improve the appeal of their religion for Westerners – specifically for British colonialists – who often looked upon Hinduism as a barbaric religion. In short, Maharishi was preaching a viewpoint close to the distilled Hinduism of earlier movements. Furthermore, his positing of an eternal philosophy implicit in nature was itself part of Hinduism. In India, one commonly hears the religion referred to as the sanatana dharma. But in TM culture, SCI was only aligned with Shankara and the holy tradition of saints who came before and after him because these saints had discovered, rather than generated, this eternal philosophy. Maharishi's teachings weren't Hinduism, or at least not *only* Hinduism. They were universal. This remains the rationale of the TM movement today.

As Maharishi's initiative of requiring a dress code intensified in the mid-1970s, his focus on the behavior of initiators increased. If they kept long hair, grew beards, or dressed in unseemly fashions, they could lose the privilege of initiating people. Furthermore, if they strayed from using the newly standardized terms of Maharishi's message, they would be reprimanded. In fact, memorizing and using the language of SCI became part of honoring the purity of the teaching and allegiance to the holy tradition. The insider view was that Maharishi knew the true purity of Shankara's message better than anyone, including India's pandits; therefore, any adjustments he made to that message must be correct. One upshot of this assumption was that Maharishi's dictates, now increasingly delivered to initiators by his functionaries in the growing organization, gained the authority of irrefutable mandates. He was the mouthpiece of nature's truth and his lieutenants were his megaphones. Conforming to this viewpoint triggered an irony soon to be shared across most guru movements in America, when a subset of the most anti-authoritarian generation in American history surrendered all authority to a single person, the guru.

Maharishi's mandates could not be questioned, and most of his teachers had no problem with that. He was enlightened and the embodiment of what he termed "spontaneous right action" (Mahesh Yogi 1969: 192), therefore, he must be saying and doing what was right. They too would soon be enlightened, but for now if they had to rely on their guru's judgment, that was only prudent. Exactly how long would it take them to become enlightened? The standard answer was five to eight years. That was the active rumor throughout the movement, and it is significant to note that neither Maharishi nor his leaders discouraged it, as our sources all agreed. In fact, well-known leaders of the organization offered the same time frame openly (see, e.g., Ebon 1975: 88). As a result, TM insiders imagined that the hundreds of thousands of people they had taught TM would quickly rise to enlightenment, becoming independent maharishis themselves. However, even if enlightenment was easily attained, how long would it take to teach TM to everyone in the world? The good news was that such an undertaking wasn't necessary. They didn't have to teach everyone; their target goal, based on a hypothesis from Maharishi, was that 10 percent would be enough.

One of Maharishi's habits each year was to go into silence for one week. When he emerged from these retreats, he delivered what might be termed a state-of-the-movement address. He had dubbed 1972 "The Year of the World Plan," and charged his movement to make TM available to as many people as possible by specifically establishing 3,600 TM centers around the globe. The world population in 1972 was 3.6 billion, so Maharishi reasoned that the best way to complete the movement's mission was to have one center for every million people. Each center would then train 100 teachers and each teacher would train 1,000 meditators to achieve the 10 percent goal. Unfortunately, within only two or three years, the guru realized the growth of the global population was far outstripping even his incredible increase in initiators; it was clear that teaching even 10 percent of the world's population was not going to happen.

Shooting for an unachievable goal would have been discouraging for his followers, but before that could occur, Maharishi had discovered something that, to critics, sounded like a convenient miracle. During a press conference in Vittel, France, Maharishi announced in 1975 that to create global utopia, it would no longer be necessary to teach 10 percent of the world to meditate. He explained that scientists at Maharishi International University (MIU) had discovered that even 1 percent would be enough; in fact, transition to this goal had already begun. (MIU first offered classes in 1973 in Santa Barbara, California, but moved in August of 1974 to Fairfield, Iowa.) Therefore, Maharishi declared 1975 as the first year of the Age of Enlightenment. While TMers were excited, many scientists, in fact all scientists who were not affiliated with the TMO, found Maharishi's pronouncement suspicious if not downright ridiculous.

The following year, 1976, Dr. David Orme-Johnson, a psychology professor at Maharishi's university, explained that additional studies he, along with Candace Borland and Garland Landrith, had performed, in the labs at MIU (e.g., Borland & Landrith 1977), substantiated the theory that having 1 percent meditating could cause what the movement soon spoke of as a "phase transition" in consciousness dubbed "The Maharishi Effect" (Aron & Aron 1986: 39, 112). This term soon became a mainstay in the movement's vernacular. This meant that just a few years after starting the World Plan, that plan was obsolete, superseded by a new program. Orme-Johnson's group seemed to provide proof – for TM insiders – that even before 10 percent learned TM, the world could blossom into peace and harmony. To that end, a new program began in 1977 titled the "One in One Hundred Campaign," designed to teach 1 percent of every country's population – in the United States the goal was to teach two million people before the end of the year. Posters were put up that read, "You can afford to be one of the 99 if you can find one of your friends to be THE ONE." This was good psychology for marketing. Who would not want to be "The One?" In today's mythos it would translate into becoming Neo from the *Matrix* series of films, the divine anomaly. Feeling that their ultimate goal was back within reach, initiators hunkered down.

Even two years earlier, in 1975, so much energy, excitement, and hoopla had been communicated to the American public that one reporter observed, "Maharishi will surely someday be awarded an honorary degree in marketing science" (White 1976: 128). The guru's publicity savvy – another kind of Maharishi Effect – was substantial. But why did Maharishi make the extravagant claim of an Age of Enlightenment just when everything was going so well? Did he really believe utopia was dawning? Or was it that he mostly hoped to squeeze more energy out of his troops? His subsequent behavior suggests it may have been a bit of both. Maharishi's work ethic could not be denied; he labored tirelessly every day, rarely even stopping for meals. Moreover, he shared manifest joy over the discoveries of his scientists since these provided signs that he was succeeding. It may be that his romanticism in the 1970s was as great as that of his followers, which, by the way, would help to explain his later cynicism about the world, and world leaders, when nothing remotely like a global utopia ever arrived. Whatever the case, his proclamation of a coming utopia clearly sabotaged his appeal with the mainstream. Not only did the Age of Enlightenment smack of religion, but it was also incredibly hard to swallow. Nobody opposed world peace in principle, but glancing at the news headlines each morning made it difficult to believe utopia had dawned.

Maharishi truly seems to have believed an upturn in world events would eventually prove him right, assuring an unbelieving press, as he did, "you'll see, you'll see." But the fact is that his proclamation heralded, and even helped precipitate, the movement's dramatic decline. The declaration cast Maharishi back into the role of deluded mystic for mainstream Americans. According to the TMO's records, about 300,000 people learned TM in 1975, and by the end of 1976 there were more than one million. But then the heyday was over.

5 TM on Trial

In 1975 and 1976, publicity for TM was everywhere and the movement was growing by leaps and bounds. In fact, so quickly that in the United States the national office, located in Pacific Palisades, California, could not coordinate all the TM-related activities for IMS and SIMS, having to rely increasingly on regional coordinators. Bobby Lee was the director for the south; Bill Witherspoon for the midwest; Stan Crowe in the west; and Charlie Donahue in the northeast, with all four reporting to Jerry Jarvis. Furthermore, the movement had now relocated its university to Fairfield, Iowa, drawing hundreds of applicants who sought a college education based on SCI. Enthusiasm among movement insiders was so strong that by the summer of 1974, the new university had already outgrown its facilities in Santa Barbara, California, causing Maharishi to purchase the abandoned campus of Parsons College in Fairfield. As we've seen, the TM movement was growing quickly. Maharishi, of course, welcomed this growth but there was certainly a downside, given that the new flock of meditators differed from his earlier followers. The new TMers had signed up to improve their health and efficiency, as promised in magazine articles, with little interest in reaching enlightenment and no interest in augmenting their religious practices with borrowings from Hinduism. Therefore, a curious result of the Merv Wave for the TM movement was that it generated a definite division in the ranks of TMers, with the mainstreamers – mostly middle-aged folks hoping for health benefits – now a far larger group than the insiders yearning for spiritual awakening. Using metrics for NRMs suggested by Bainbridge and Stark, these TMers fit best into the client cult category of their entrepreneur model, a model in which the clientele is made up of customers consuming a product for a fee and not counted upon to become "full members of the organization" (Bainbridge & Stark 2003: 64). Transcendental Meditation insiders, however, fit easily inside Bainbridge and Stark's subculture-evolution model, in which more complex rewards or compensators are involved, including the addition of a new ideological outlook and stronger social ties (Bainbridge & Stark 2005: 67).

Scientific legitimization, health-based personal goals, and faddism had created a wave of meditators with little understanding of, or attraction to, enticements of a spiritual sort, sometimes causing a disconnect between mainstreamers and insiders. Mainstreamers were doing TM to lower their blood pressure or relieve ulcers, to perform better in class, and to increase their productivity at work or reduce sick leave, and whole sports teams learned meditation to gain an edge on winning. But where did spiritual seekers fit into that equation? Many insiders wondered. The spin-doctoring had brought in dizzying numbers of recruits, but it placed the early wave of TMers in a minority position, who often felt more like exiles than leaders of their own movement, though it seemed best – for the sake of creating utopia – to stay in the movement.

In 1976, the TMO, spurred on by its new initiatives, aggressively attempted to introduce meditation into public secondary schools in America, having already received scores of governmental proclamations supporting that attempt. Interest in TM from educators had been accumulating since early 1972. In October of that year, Francis Driscoll, Superintendent of Schools for Eastchester, New York, wrote "the practice of meditation possesses considerable promise for students of high school age," adding descriptions of the positive effects of TM he had witnessed in his own schools (Driscoll 1972: 236). Other prominent educators also gave endorsements, including Max Raines, professor of higher education at Michigan State University, Dean Brown, director of the Educational Technology Project at Stanford Research Institute, and Conrad F. Toepfer, Jr., associate professor of education at the State University of New York at Buffalo. When these letters and articles were brought to Maharishi's attention, he reasoned that if public schools implemented TM, it would become institutionalized, bringing TM to every child in America and fulfilling the World Plan there overnight. This was the sort of delivery engine Maharishi had hoped for, and though it may seem unlikely today, the effort nearly succeeded.

In 1975, Maharishi and TMO leaders cheered when they learned federal funds had been awarded for a Title III Education Research Program to investigate the benefits of TM in six New Jersey schools. However, the project was diligently opposed by two unlikely bedfellows: conservative Christians, outraged by what they saw as a surreptitious insinuation of Hinduism into public education, and staunch secularists, worried that SCI was a religion in disguise. When the opposition prepared to file a lawsuit, the TMO realized the situation was serious. They had already lost a legal battle in San Lorenzo, California, in 1973, running up against the same separation of church and state principle. In addition, just the year before, an attempt to secure a proclamation of support for TM from the state legislature of New Jersey (Assembly Resolution 47) had failed, detractors arguing that TM was an offshoot of Hinduism. Consequently, the new legal battle would be decisive, establishing a strong precedent. The TMO had to do whatever it could to keep from being perceived as religious. Just before the case went to trial, TM initiators received a private memo from Lenny Goldman, chief attorney for the TMO, explaining the proper legal use of the term TM. It had been loosely used before – sometimes describing a program, sometimes a technique, and sometimes the SCI philosophy – but now teachers were advised to be specific. They should describe meditation as the "TM technique" and Maharishi's philosophy as the SCI, with two specific goals: clarity and secular appeal.

Additional memos came down from headquarters urging initiators to appear nonreligious by refraining from saying Jai Guru Dev ("Hail, O Divine Teacher") in public and putting away their devotional pictures of Maharishi. Initiators affiliated with IMS and SIMS quickly conformed with these policies, but SRM insiders kept up their spiritual focus, with their leader, Charlie Lutes, continuing to claim he had seen angels and UFOs, and that space aliens supported Maharishi's World Plan efforts. Jon Michael Miller, the host of a talk show on the TM television channel KSCI, later reported his exasperation with Lutes, commenting that "reining in Charlie Lutes' mind was like corralling wild mustangs" (Miller 2006: 212–3). The good news for Maharishi was that the court seemed unaware of Lutes.

The plaintiffs in the suit included an unincorporated association known as the Coalition for Religious Integrity, consisting of eight taxpayers, a New Jersey clergyman, and members of Americans United for Separation of Church and State. Together they were suing not only the TMO but also the State of New Jersey, the US Department of Health, Education and Welfare, and, last but not least, the United States itself. In *Alan B. Malnak, et al.,* v. *Maharishi Mahesh Yogi, et al.,* these plaintiffs moved for summary judgment to prevent teaching TM in public schools on the grounds that doing so would violate the First Amendment. The primary tactic of the defense was to claim that meditators did not relate to Maharishi's teachings as religious – which was literally true for the mainstreamers. The court considered this defense, but when it issued its decision on December 1, 1977, the judgment was that "subjective characterizations of actions and beliefs as religious or scientific or philosophical will vary among individuals because of their varying concepts of religion or science or philosophy." Accordingly, the court refused to be put in a position of having to examine or accept the intellectual classification system of each individual meditator. Its reasoning was that if sincerity set the standard, religion under the First Amendment would take on a different meaning in every conceivable court case, and similar or virtually identical practices could be religious or not depending on subjective viewpoints. This was considered a slippery slope in a secular democracy. In no time at all, Baptists, Catholics, and Hare Krishnas would be in court claiming they were not religious either, and thus be eligible for public financial support. The judges also noted (to Maharishi's chagrin) that they were in fact aware of Lutes and the SRM, pointing out, "Until 1965, the Spiritual Regeneration Movement Foundation was the only organization in the United States that offered instruction in Maharishi Mahesh Yogi's teachings. . . . [And] one of the articles of the certificate of incorporation, as amended, of the SRM Foundation stated that 'this corporation is a religious one'" (*TM in Court* 1978: 58). The court accepted this as an admission of guilt, and so, in the decision filed by the District Justice, the Honorable Curtis Meanor, the plaintiffs won on all counts.

Now that the court had established a legal precedent for labeling TM a religious practice, it hindered all attempts by the TMO to gain government support for its programs. The delivery engine Maharishi had hoped would produce the Age of Enlightenment had fizzled, and a major transition in public response to his mission quickly followed. John White's articles of that time reflect the trend (White 1976). But Maharishi, who was still touring to herald the Age of Enlightenment, was publicly unfazed by the court's ruling (Oates 1976). According to insiders, he was privately deeply upset, moving his attention immediately toward other projects – particularly a new program he hoped would quickly boost meditators into enlightenment. This new program, the TM-Sidhis Program, constitutes a critical stage in the TM movement's history because it helped precipitate the end of the TM movement's meteoric rise. The Sidhis, in tribute to the *siddhis* or "supernatural powers" described in Patanjali's *Yoga Sutras*, became the new focus of all activities, forming a distraction for insiders from the recent defeat in New Jersey, while also providing a needed revenue stream, since initiations into TM had begun to plummet.

Insiders wondered at the need to experiment with new techniques when Maharishi had already explained that TM was the fastest method of spiritual growth. Maharishi explained: the new techniques involved mentally repeating certain of Patanjali's sutras related to such remarkable abilities as materializing objects, speaking with animals, becoming invisible, reading minds, seeing into the past, foretelling the future, levitating in space, and more, but the goal was not to achieve these abilities so much as to generate a state of consciousness in which the Absolute would be pulled into one's everyday state of mind, forwarding one's growth to enlightenment. In terms of the process itself, meditators would first practice TM and then spend another fifteen minutes holding their attention on a set of sutras one at a time.

Critics then, and in the years ahead, characterized the new program as a diversion from TM or worse, simply another product to sell. Others believed Maharishi's motivation for the program stemmed from his hope that if his followers demonstrated extraordinary abilities, the public would have to believe his programs worked – a modern manifestation of Christ's position that his miracles legitimated his divinity (John 10: 38). But this begged the question: Why couldn't Maharishi, whom everyone in the movement considered enlightened, simply perform the miracles himself? Movement leaders, urged by Maharishi, responded that if he did so, the public would get the wrong impression. They would think only Maharishi was capable of such feats, whereas if hundreds of mediators did something impossible, the world would have to accept that the program worked.

The early trials were disappointing, given that nobody in the courses seemed capable of doing anything remotely magical. The greatest success – measured by the fact that at least *something* happened – occurred when the practitioners focused on the sutra for yogic flying. These folks babbled, grimaced, laughed, twitched, and sometimes hopped around. From the outside, such behavior didn't seem like much of a triumph, but Maharishi argued it was just a matter of time before the little hops turned into full-blown levitation. Maharishi once again began telling his initiators that success was just ahead and that science was on their side, so, as Goldberg has written, the "TM reps" felt "certain that their claims would soon be validated" (Goldberg 2010: 170).

In late 1977, movement scientists, including Keith Wallace, Michael Dilbeck, and David Orme-Johnson, shared preliminary in-house studies, purporting that during the performance of the Sidhis, and especially while using the flying sutra, brainwave coherence in test subjects had increased markedly – even higher than the levels registered during TM (see Orme-Johnson et al. 1978, 1981). It was not, and is not, an established fact that increasing coherence between the hemispheres of the brain is actually an improvement, but conventional wisdom in psychology at that time maintained it was, so Maharishi's scientists speculated this increased coherence would accelerate the Maharishi Effect. Two TM insiders shared the official description of the effect: "When a small proportion of a population or a group is in a highly ordered state, then the whole group will become highly ordered" (Robins & Himber 1976: 129). Prior to 1977, this required "small proportion," as we've seen, was 1 percent, but the new evidence coming from MIU suggested the small proportion might be only a fraction of 1 percent if people practiced the Sidhis. Based on theories derived from quantum physics, offered to Maharishi by Lawrence Domash, a follower who was also a physics professor at Amherst College, researchers at MIU sought out what this fraction might be.

Many initiators, including Jerry Jarvis, Charlie Donahue, and other high-ranking officials, were skeptical, if not of the new program itself then of the rationale of shifting attention from TM and the World Plan. Why reduce the ranks of initiators offering TM to the public by sending them away to learn the Sidhis? What if the new brainwave coherence studies were inconclusive? How certain was this new requisite percentage for creating "global coherence?" If the movement's goal was to help the world, and TM was proven effective for improving the lives of the people who made it up, weren't initiation figures the most objective and reliable way to monitor success? Differences of opinion over the best way to proceed began to divide the body of TM insiders. While the majority was inclined to agree with Maharishi, or to set their doubts aside, a significant number stayed focused on teaching TM and avoided the new program. Those who followed Maharishi's line were sometimes sympathetic to the holdouts but could never support going against Maharishi. Detractors shared their worry that Maharishi's thinking was now being disastrously influenced by sycophants, including movement scientists jockeying for position. Many suspected that the decisions they disliked, handed down "from Maharishi," actually originated with one or another movement underling. This was a primary rationale for holdouts not backing the Sidhis program. Sympathy for the holdouts among their fellow initiators increased once news of the Sidhis was released to the public.

In 1977, movement press releases featured a photograph of cross-legged meditators hanging in the air, reputedly increasing their brainwave coherence by means of yogic hopping. Underneath the photo, the caption read, "The higher they go, the happier they become." But the yogis were not the only ones smiling. Soon Maharishi was showing up on the cover of *The Enquirer* and *The Weekly World News* rather than the cover of *Time.* To make matters worse, the credibility of gurus in general had plummeted over the past couple of years, with the press eager to play the role of cynic. Scandals involving a fifteen-year-old religious leader named Guru Maharaj-ji, accused of sleeping with his secretary, and Sun Myung Moon, the Korean founder of the Unification Church (also called pejoratively the Moonies) accused of brainwashing his disciples, filled the news. This was one of the fiercest years of the anticult movement and it helped turn the media's critical eye on Maharishi. But the guru, according to videotaped reports regularly sent to his followers, remained unperturbed. His faith in the power of the Sidhis was so unshakable he was willing to be a punching bag for the press. For the first time in his career, he seemed to stop trying to control the media's image of him. Armed with a new and more potent program, he would create the global Maharishi Effect using only those from within his own group, fulfilling the World Plan from the inside out. If he could recruit the requisite number of meditators to learn the "Maharishi Technology of the Unified Field" – the new name for his TM-Sidhis Program – he could effect the desired phase transition. He would get the world population to change whether they liked it or not, pushed forward by the sheer force of the brain coherence among his sidhas. Maharishi therefore instructed his teachers to promote attending Sidhis courses over going to TTCs; the world already had enough meditators, now it needed sidhas (the movement name for those who practice the Sidhis program).

In 1978, research by MIU scientists indicated that brainwave coherence increased even more when sidhas practiced in the same location, setting off a new wave of excitement in the TMO because any increase in coherence was instantly interpreted as suggesting the "small proportion" needed to generate utopia could be reduced proportionally (Aron & Aron 1986: 112). The theory was that doing the program together created a synergistic effect so great that only a few thousand sidhas pooled up in only a handful of locations might be enough. The theory of this effect was quickly accepted and dubbed in movement literature "Super Radiance." Goldberg comments that the presumption was that "orderly EEG waves generated by individuals" would be "amplified geometrically" and the coherence radiated outward "like broadcast signals" (Goldberg 2010: 170). According to a movement pamphlet, the effect was similar to Super Radiance in physical systems such as lasers when the coherent elements of a system emit a powerfully coherent light. This analogy was used repeatedly in movement literature and an explanation of it is given in Aron and Aron (1986: 111–2). Soon movement scientists theorized that the fraction of the population needed to generate utopia could be reduced to the square root of 1 percent, and this became their newest mathematical formula for global salvation

In the summer of 1978, Maharishi's "Year of Ideal Society," the TMO sought to prove statistically its quantum-based theory of the Maharishi Effect by launching studies in states with high populations of TMers. Rhode Island and Washington were the best candidates, so the plan was to move large numbers of initiators into those states to push the number of meditators over the 1 percent mark. During the Ideal Society Campaign, Rhode Island was the state focused on by TM scientists to yield the necessary statistical data (Aron & Aron 1986: 59). Walter Zimmerman, a movement researcher (no outside scientists were involved), monitored twenty-one variables and later claimed Rhode Island had indeed experienced a 28 percent improvement in outcomes from the previous five summers (Aron & Aron 1986: 60). For Maharishi and TMO officials, Zimmerman's study was sufficiently significant to confirm the Super Radiance Effect, so they stopped speaking of their theories as analogous to those of quantum physics; they were the expressions of quantum physics itself.

In January 1979, Maharishi announced he would fully deploy Super Radiance by creating "Ideal Villages" on several continents where sidhas could practice together. Only four of these would generate enough Super Radiance to reach every corner of the globe. Scientific studies would then encourage more sidhas to move to the Ideal Villages, plus encourage more meditators to become sidhas. However, scientists outside the TMO had serious doubts about the conclusions of the Rhode Island study – the very study upon which so many of the TM movements' current plans depended, and those doubts grew stronger in the years ahead.

6 A Taste of Utopia and a Return to the Vedas

In the United States, the Ideal Village was located in and around MIU in Iowa, given that it already had the largest concentration of sidhas in the world. During a month-long course in summer 1979 at the University of Massachusetts, Amherst, Maharishi phoned in to deliver just one message: "Move to Fairfield." That fall the most zealous of American TMers did just that, moving in with old friends until they could figure out how to support themselves. Living conditions were often cramped or otherwise difficult, but their faith in the new project kept them optimistic. Buttressing that optimism, Maharishi declared that a new hall would be built for practicing together, and in December, work began on a golden-roofed dome, called the Maharishi Patanjali Golden Dome of Pure Knowledge. It was inaugurated in spring 1980, and soon another dome was constructed to maintain separation of the sexes. TMers thought construction of these distinctive domes glorious, but local Iowans were often scathing in their assessment, popularly lampooning the domes as the "Dolly Parton Monument."

In December 1983, Maharishi came to Fairfield to attend a two-week "Taste of Utopia" conference, hoping to encourage more TMers to move to Iowa, given that the requisite number of sidhas hadn't yet been reached. TMers would visit the Ideal Village and get a taste of what they could experience full time if they moved there. In addition, via the conference the world would get a glimpse of paradise through the Super Radiance being broadcast. Thousands attended – estimates from attendees range from 5,000 to 8,000 – but relatively few stayed. In 1980, the TMO estimated that the number of sidhas required to generate the necessary Super Radiance Effect was 1,800, but such a number was never achieved for more than brief periods, and since that time, as world population has increased, the required number has risen.

Many initiators chose to leave the TMO in the late 1970s and early 1980s. They had believed TM was the fastest way to evolve spiritually, and they had dedicated themselves to teaching as many people as possible. The new program and its tendency to make the movement inwardly focused disturbed them. Or as Jerry Jarvis once remarked to a regional coordinator, "The movement has turned in on itself in an unhealthy way."[2] But the largest number of insiders who left the organization at that time simply did so because they hoped to start a family or find a stable occupation, initiatives they had postponed for years out of devotion to the movement.

For most who remained, the TM-Sidhis Program, the Ideal Society Campaign, and the Ideal Village Project constituted a logical progression, revealing both the brilliance and nimbleness of Maharishi's mind. But outside observers generally viewed these programs as the cause of the TMO's slide into obscurity. In terms of new initiations into TM, Maharishi had basically dismantled his own movement in just three years. Whatever the case, by the spring of 1980 the TMO as a publicly focused educational organization had largely ceased to exist. The organization kept its ultimate goal in place – to spiritually regenerate the world – but for the first time in more than twenty years, its method for achieving that goal was no longer exclusively TM. Maharishi had reduced his ranks to those most convinced of his new plans, and it's worth noting that during this period the TMO lost many of its best and brightest. Furthermore, even among those who were enthusiastic about Maharishi's plans, there were many who could not leave their jobs, families, or hometowns to relocate to the corn belt. They would practice the new program at their local TM centers, resigned to the fact they were being less effective than Maharishi wished them to be.

In the 1980s, the TMO was mostly interested in teaching its own members the new program, with TM centers rapidly evaporating from the landscape. Where once there had been more than 400 TM centers in the United States, there were now fewer than 60. And given that it was no longer necessary to interact with the public or the press, the TMO began to adopt what many in both the organization and the public interpreted as absurdly grandiose titles for its leaders and functionaries. Neil Patterson, a monk who was officiating at the TMO's Livingston Manor facility in upstate New York, was promoted to the position of Governor General of the Age of Enlightenment for North America. There was also a cadre of TM nuns collectively called Mother Divine. Soon there was an organizational hierarchy tantamount to the Indian caste system, comprised of – in order of ascension – meditators, citizen sidhas, governors, governor generals, ministers, chancellors, and eventually also rajas and a maharaja.

Peter McWilliams, a former TMer, offered a dark but plausible rationale for why the TMO turned inward. He asserted that TM had been taught as a "simple,

---

[2] Informant wishes to remain anonymous.

twenty-minute, twice-a-day technique that would, in eight years of regular practice, lead to Cosmic Consciousness." He practiced it "for precisely eight years – without missing a single meditation – did not achieve Cosmic Consciousness, and stopped" (McWilliams 1994: 407). In McWilliams' opinion, Maharishi intentionally developed the Sidhi Program "to turn off the casual meditator while drawing the devout believers closer to him" (McWilliams 1994: 410). Exactly how many ordinary meditators left the movement at this time is difficult to say, given that there was no formal membership program and most TMers kept no strong ties with the formal organization. These mainstreamers fit most easily into Bainbridge and Stark's audience cult or client cult categories, and they have continued to drift off the radar. Some continue to meditate – even after forty years or more – while most are likely to have lost interest over time.

Returning to circumstances in Fairfield, in the early 1980s there was a deep sense of camaraderie, with MIU now presided over by Lawrence Domash, acting president, and Bevan Morris, a young Australian in charge of the Town Super Radiance Program. As in all religions or societies sharing a common worldview – whether Mormons, Moonies, Muslims, or Marxists – the vast majority of TMers in Fairfield experienced a collective sense of meaning and purpose that is uncommon in the Western world today. They shared each others' values and made sense of the world in nearly identical ways. To convey a picture of this group identity and its definite rewards (both social and personal), a key informant wrote in a memoir of her life in Fairfield, where she lived for eleven years:

> I loved my routine [of going to the dome everyday] and above all seeing so many friends with common ideals trying to create a better situation for peace in the world. Each afternoon I'd walk across the foam mattresses that lined the meditation hall floor, settle into my seat, wrap up in a shawl and just before closing my eyes for an hour or two, see some dear companions do the same. Afterwards we would chat as we strolled out to our cars to make our way back home.

Those who eventually left the Ideal Village reported disappointment over how things had developed. They remembered it was difficult to support themselves; that the necessary number of meditators had never arrived; that the winters were cold and wet; that the locals weren't always friendly to those they called "Roos" (short for "Goo-Roos"); and that the organization's structure had become too authoritarian. Initiators had once enjoyed nearly as much autonomy from the formal organization as the mainstreamers who learned TM and then practiced on their own. According to McCutchan, TM teachers "were simply exhorted to 'do what you know is right and don't do what you know is wrong'"

(McCutchan 1977: 147). Beyond that, initiators had set up their own TM courses for the public, hosted their own advanced lectures, and kept their own council. They operated independently and on commission like vacuum cleaner salesmen or vitamin distributors. But when the organization turned inward, and when insiders convened in Fairfield, this changed. Now they were required to register for admission to the domes, wearing identity badges to get inside, and understood that they must follow rules or lose their badges. Increasingly, from McCutchan's perspective, "what had begun as a 'religion of ecstasy' had become a 'religion of control'" (McCutchan 1977: 147). The dress code now included an institutional element, with designated dress – suits for men and matronly dresses for women – showing solidarity with the group.

Some measure of the institutional hierarchy that caused many insiders to leave – or to not move to Fairfield in the first place – began with Maharishi's cultural propensities. As early as 1971, he had begun surrounding himself with novice monks, a group that included Robert McCutchan, Casey Coleman, Billy Clayton, Shannon Dickson, Lewis Dyson, Russell Hebert, William Frills, and, a bit later, John Gray (author of *Men are from Mars, Women are from Venus*). These *braahmacaris* (student monks) practiced celibacy and preserved a code of asceticism common to Hindu culture, and their elevation in status, signified by their closeness to the guru, revealed Maharishi's acceptance of forms famil- iar to Hinduism. In accordance with this, Maharishi dictated all aspects of their lives, even deciding what clothes they should wear and what food they should eat. Collectively, they were commonly called "skin boys" because these young men carried the deer skin upon which Maharishi sat when giving lectures.

At the movement's height, a system of regional leaders was overseen by national leaders who reported directly to Maharishi, with all attention focused outwardly. But after the movement turned in on itself, the mostly autonomous initiators who dealt with the public were no longer necessary or desired; it was better for them to move to an Ideal Village and contribute to Super Radiance. Therefore, the highest officials of the organization after the early 1980s were the bureaucrats running the Ideal Villages, answering in turn to Maharishi and his "ministers" on international staff. All of these functionaries were arranged in a hierarchical order, passing down Maharishi's directives through a chain of command at each level of authority and with little chance to offer any element of loyal opposition. Each level of functionaries obeyed the dictates of its superiors, with behaviors, beliefs, and institutional language increasingly rigid in form. This was based on the presumption that such rigidity preserved the purity of the teaching, which was at that point synonymous with Maharishi's directives.

As noted, the primary reason why TM insiders left concerned issues of occupation and family, but as we've also seen, there were disgruntled practitioners who departed because of changes in the movement. During the 1980s and beyond, TM increasingly became only one product in a spectrum of therapies. In addition to the Sidhis, other opportunities, pitched to insiders as enormously beneficial to their health and spiritual growth, were revealed by Maharishi with the regularity and status that in the twenty-first century accompany the announcement of new iPhones. This pleased some, eager to accept any recommendation from Maharishi, but others felt the constant offerings smacked of blatant commercialism. Adding so many new products felt like a bait and switch maneuver, since Maharishi had claimed for years that TM was all that was needed to reach enlightenment. In addition, these new programs – collectively falling under the banner of what Maharishi termed Vedic Science – aligned the movement more and more with Hinduism, compromising Maharishi's original claim that the movement was nonreligious.

In the late 1970s, Maharishi had begun associating TM and his other so-called scientific techniques with the Vedic worldview of his native India. His emerging plan was to finance the glorification of Vedic culture, and then act as a bridge to bring its revitalized wisdom to the rest of the world. Acting as guinea pigs, TMers would first test the ideas and products Maharishi developed and then help him promote what worked best. In the early 1980s, they accepted treatments based on Ayur Veda (traditional Indian medicine) along with Hindu dietary preferences. Indian pandits, with expertise in Hindu *jyotish* (astrology), *yagya* (ceremonies to secure "the support of nature"), and *Gandharva Veda* (a textbook of Hindu musicology), were courted and added to TMO's payroll. One Ayur Veda pandit in particular became a special favorite of Maharishi and had great influence on the direction of the movement in the days to come. A heavy-set, charismatic physician named Brihaspati Dev Triguna, or Triguna Ji, went into business with Maharishi, producing remedies and preventives from his own recipes. Transcendental Meditation insiders began testing his products, spooning up an antioxidant elixir called Maharishi Amrit Kalash ("Maharishi's Pot of Immortal Ambrosia") as a staple of their diet. To help with this initiative, Deepak Chopra, an Indian-born and Western-trained physician, apprenticed with Triguna to better promote "Maharishi Ayur Veda" the trademarked brand.

To provide a curriculum and teaching venue for all the new programs, in 1980 Maharishi decided to create a Vedic university in India, establishing it on land initially purchased for an ashram. Maharishi Nagar, the "City of Maharishi," was located in the New Okhla Industrial Development Area (Noida) on the outskirts of Delhi. At first, Maharishi's city began as little more than a group of dusty tents and a line of crude latrines. To develop the project further, the guru needed funding. He therefore invited all his followers to a World Assembly on Vedic Science in India, assuring them that this event would be the next giant step in their personal growth. For many insiders, this would not only be an opportunity to see Maharishi but also to visit India, the birthplace of the movement.

Maharishi had returned home to reaffirm the supremacy of India's indigenous truths, and the World Assembly would showcase those truths. He had once written, as the first sentence in his commentary on the Bhagavad Gita, "The Vedas are the lighthouse of eternal wisdom leading man to salvation and inspiring him to supreme accomplishment" (Mahesh Yogi 1969: 9), and now he would tout that culture-specific message in a giant assembly. Western physics had provided Maharishi with scientific vocabulary, but in 1980, he asserted that that knowledge was available in Vedic Science. When, in the future, Western science completed itself, it would realize it had actually only reinvented a wheel that had existed in India for eons. This was the general message of the gathering.

The assembly was promoted as an investigation into the presumed correspondence between Vedic Science and modern science, and it took place in November, during the Hindu festival of Diwali, with perhaps 2,500 TMers in attendance; most were Westerners. There were daily lectures held in the vacant spaces of the *Indian Express* building, but the assembly also included an experiential component, or it had intended to do so. Maharishi had hired hundreds of pandits to participate in a giant *yagya* ceremony, with the plan that they would sit in the center of a huge mandala (spiritual circle) and chant verses from the Vedas while thousands of TMers simultaneously meditated in a ring around them. This yagya, Maharishi attested, would generate a super-Super Radiance effect, or as he described it in the *Sunday Standard*, "an intense influence of *sattva* [life force] for the entire world's population to enjoy" (Mahesh Yogi 1969: 9). To his chagrin, however, problems confounded the ceremony, including the fact that most of the Westerners fell sick soon after arrival. Their illnesses, including dysentery, were not serious in most cases, but the breakout resulted in postponement of the yagyas.

Another problem at the World Assembly on Vedic Science concerned the caliber of pandits who had been hired for the yagya ceremonies. A few months before the conference, Maharishi had met Sri Sri Ravi Shankar (b. 1956) in Bangalore, during a symposium to discuss Veda and science; thereafter he asked Sri Sri (as he is known to followers) to represent him as a proxy during visits to various ashrams in India. When the World Assembly in Delhi held its first puja ceremony to welcome the pandits, a virtual riot had occurred when the pandits rushed for the sweets on offer. Consequently, Maharishi asked Sri Sri to look into the reasons for such behavior. The result was that Sri Sri discovered that kickbacks had been received by Maharishi's Indian devotees who had recruited the pandits – many of whom were actually fakes (Gautier 2008: 37–38). Not a single one of the scheduled yagyas ever took place during the assembly and, given the number of unqualified pandits, likely would not have occurred even if Maharishi's Western followers hadn't taken ill.

For press coverage throughout the assembly, Maharishi characteristically put a happy face on matters, keeping up a cheery mood. Perhaps any disappointment he may have felt was tempered by the fact that he had reaffirmed his Hindu roots. Moreover, Tony Nader, a Lebanese neurophysiologist, emerged during the assembly as a bright personality interested in drawing parallels between Western science and Eastern wisdom. Years later, Maharishi would proclaim Nader the maharaja of the territory of the unified field and "First Sovereign Ruler of the Global Country of World Peace" (Siegel 2018: 65). Today Nader is the leader of the international TMO.

7 Gurus Who Broke from Maharishi

Only a few years after Swami Brahmananda's death, Maharishi positioned his method of meditation as the legitimate, authentic, and genuine heir to an ancient practice from a tradition of well-recognized and respected teachers (Lewis 2003: 15). This alignment with the holy tradition of Shankara was routinely cited by Maharishi as a sacred trust, not to be broken by heterodox views or schism, defined in the TMO as any deviance from Maharishi's thoughts or directives. But in the 1980s, Maharishi, for the first time since his fiasco with the London followers of Gurdjieff and Ouspensky, experienced two primary challenges to his authority.

As the TM movement in the United States stumbled, rival gurus sought to repackage the insights they had gleaned from the organization. One of the two most notable, and notorious, of the rival gurus was Robin Woodsworth Carlsen, a Canadian initiator who claimed he had reached perfect enlightenment in Arosa, Switzerland, while attending an advanced course for TM initiators. According to his written account, Carlsen had announced his enlightenment during an evening meeting and Maharishi had acknowledged it (Carlsen 1979: 11). But when he returned to British Columbia with the happy news, his fellow initiators weren't convinced of his claim, nor did they believe that Maharishi wished him to steer the organization's teachings in a new direction.

Carlsen explained he could engage with TMers on the level of their individual psyches to help them improve and purify the raw dimensions of their minds while also aligning those dimensions with the Self/Brahman/Pure Creative Intelligence accessed via TM. In this regard, he would use techniques borrowed from his earlier guru, Werner Erhard, the founder of Erhard Seminar Training (est) (Humes 2009: 287–305). Carlsen began employing confrontational techniques with a few converts, pressuring them in various ways in order to trigger the release of their psychological, emotional, and spiritual habits and baggage, including those incurred by demonic possession (Humes 2009: 287–305). He secured few recruits in Canada, so he decided to move to Fairfield, where there was a larger audience. On arrival, he promised to bring back what he claimed was the heart missing from the robotic hierarchy institutionalized at MIU by "Bevan's Boys," those influenced by Bevan Morris. This intrigued many local TMers. Ty Gale, an erstwhile follower, told the authors that "Robin Carlsen offered something exciting, very different. He offered new techniques of meditation, and in our imagination, they were much more powerful, and we were sucked in. In a sense, it was the opposite of the TM Movement: something quite alive."

Officials at MIU quickly tried to muzzle Carlsen although no word against him had yet come down from Maharishi, even after Carlsen began criticizing movement leaders (Carlsen 1979: 53–5). Carlsen was then banned from the MIU campus, and TMers in town were advised to shun him. But Carlsen contended that he was a living voice out of the Absolute, just like Maharishi, and therefore incapable of going against either the purity of the teaching or the will of the universe. Leaders at MIU, thinking Carlsen psychotic, narcissistic or both, repeatedly wrote to Maharishi begging him to reject Carlsen, but word was slow in coming, which Carlsen took as evidence his World Teacher Seminars were on the right track. As a result, in September 1982, Carlsen sent a letter to Greg Wilson, the TM-Sidhis coordinator at MIU, informing him that he would cease his critical agitations if Wilson could produce an official document from Maharishi asking that he should. To Carlsen's chagrin, in July 1983, Maharishi complied with the request, assessing the outlier in very negative terms. He declared that Carlsen was not enlightened and that he was deviating from the purity of the teachings. Maharishi also explicitly said that he did not want his followers to attend Carlsen's World Teacher Seminars. Carlsen was devastated, and lacking Maharishi's support, his stock quickly plummeted. He would continue to write and teach but never again worry TM officials. In fact, he became for them the poster child for the importance of "staying on the program."

The next of these early schisms, occurring almost simultaneously with Carlsen's, involved Sri Sri Ravi Shankar, though his departure was far less confrontational. Sri Sri became a devotee of Maharishi in the late 1970s. After Maharishi's Vedic Science assembly in Delhi, he was asked by his guru to establish a Vedic school in Bangalore. In 1981, Sri Sri dutifully set up Ved Vignan Maha Vidya Peeth, a boy's school of 200 children, all from the state of Karnataka. A legal trust was set up in cooperation with the Bangalore city mayor, Justice V. R. Krishna Iyer, Justice P. N. Bhagawati, and others, and for two years, the school operated smoothly. But then, according to Francois Gautier's biography of Sri Sri, "as was often the case, the TM movement soon decided to close the schools and take all the students to Delhi" (Gautier 2008: 42). This decision proved disastrous, reputedly because the students' parents disagreed with Maharishi's decision to take their children hundreds of miles from home to a city with a different language, culture, and food. Rather than comply with Maharishi's directive, Sri Sri kept the school going without his guru's help or permission, gaining the support not only of the school's parents but also the local community. Sri Sri's refusal to do as Maharishi had asked, along with his ability to raise funds on his own, led to a crisis in the Indian branch of the TM movement.

Sri Sri was then only twenty-five years old, but he began to make his own way. As a first step, he entered a period of silence for ten days to determine his next move, and when he emerged he created the Art of Living Foundation. Sri Sri claimed that during his silence he had been given a vision of a method of rhythmical breathing called Sudarshan Kriya. Other inspirations would follow and soon his followers were calling him Guruji and Guru Dev, leaving the Indian TM movement behind. But Sri Sri never discredited his old guru; in fact, he lauded Maharishi as an enlightened master, partially responsible for his own awakening. Moreover, although Sri Sri started a new organization, his message and teachings were, and are, nearly identical to Maharishi's, both conforming to the distilled core of Advaita Vedanta inherited from the works of Ram Mohan Roy, Debendranath Tagore, Swami Vivekananda, and others.

In leaving Maharishi's movement, Sri Sri took with him the blueprint of a successful mission, nearly identical in character but with the Indian-friendly additions of guru worship and bhakti practices, including the singing of bhajans (devotional hymns) during his evening satsangs (teaching sessions). Sri Sri explained to his devotees that such practices help develop an egoless Divine Love for one another as well as the guru, and his teachings resonated. He toured India with great success, and in 1983 offered his first Art of Living course in the West, in Switzerland, tapping the same audience as had Maharishi. In 1986, he traveled to California to give his first course in the United States, where Sri Sri, with his long hair, flowing beard, and white-robed appearance, seemed nearly a clone of Maharishi.

While he did not clothe his teachings in scientific garb, Sri Sri's Sahaj Samadhi Meditation, a mantric meditation performed twenty minutes twice per day, is clearly reminiscent of TM. Indeed, the description and promises of Sahaj Samadhi Meditation in promotional brochures are akin to those claimed for TM: "[it] is a unique and ancient method of personal growth," "simple and easy to learn and to practice," which "reduces stress and deepens appreciation of life," taught "personally suited to each one's needs by a local teacher." Maharishi was being rebottled, even as he had once rebottled a traditional meditation practice of his Shankara lineage. Furthermore, Sri Sri had taken Maharishi's return to Vedic authority one step further, dropping all pretense that he was teaching something other than a form of streamlined Hinduism, which made him an instant celebrity in the Indian press. How did Maharishi react to this schism? In the 1980s, Sri Sri was viewed by the TMO, with Maharishi's approval, as a kindred spirit and tolerated apostate.

Those who stood by Maharishi in the early 1980s sometimes accused those who flirted with the teachings of Sri Sri or other gurus of being fair-weather disciples, not willing to commit themselves to Maharishi. Those who visited other teachers and kept their own counsel reminded their critics that the movement had never, at least overtly, been about committing oneself to *any* guru. Nor was their practice about converting to what seemed to be turning into a surprisingly conservative form of Neo-Hinduism. Clearly, Maharishi's initiatives relative to Vedic Science, Ayur Veda, and the supremacy of knowledge in the Vedas – Hinduism's most sacred texts – indicated a general realignment with Hinduism. For many living in Fairfield, the running joke that MIU's acronym really stood for "Mostly Indian Underneath" now seemed a reality. In support of that estimation, Maharishi's loyalists had moved implicitly toward emulating the Hindu model of spiritual leadership. As *Manu Smriti*, a primary text of Hindu sacred law, mandates: "Let him never offend the teacher who initiated him" (ch. 4, vs. 162). Not to follow Maharishi's lead was to question his vision and authority, a position unconscionable for his loyal insiders, but one that now was driving others away.

After the majority of TM centers closed, and after the departures from Fairfield in the mid-1980s, the TMO – increasingly distanced from the meditators of the TM movement – became not only more Hindu but more insular (Lowe 2010: 54–76)). This left mainly loyal subjects, true believers, and autocrats to run the show. This group, whom Scott Lowe, once an insider himself, has identified as a "self-selected, relatively small group of dedicated followers" (Lowe 2010: 54), privileged Vedic Science over science itself, setting the latter inside the former. The movement's official language became ponderous and cryptic, relying on terms borrowed from theoretical physics, Hindu philosophy, and Sanskrit texts. Gone were the simple, straightforward explanations Maharishi had once used to capture the imagination of a generation. These were replaced with expressions that seemed more at home in physics textbooks or – when mixed up with the Vedic terminology – in Lewis Carroll's *Jabberwocky*.

Having "Governors and Sidhas of the Age of Enlightenment" talking about the "self-referral state of consciousness" experienced during the practice of the "Maharishi Technology of the Unified Field" was a bridge too far. In the past, groupthink had manifested to some extent in the movement but it had never been so divorced from the terms of everyday life. In the opinion of a former TMO official who wishes to remain anonymous, the TMO's language had become "a convoluted lexicon of mongrel Sanskrit scientism." The general public, already alienated from the new version of the TM movement, was being pushed even further away. But for many who stayed in Fairfield this didn't matter. If TMers could bring together a large group of "flyers" to Super Radiate, they would soon show the world the soundness of their "crazy" terms and ideas. Moreover, Maharishi's new audience, consuming his line of Ayur Veda treatments, elixirs, and food supplements, was causing a stir due to the efforts of Maharishi's new star pupil, Deepak Chopra.

8 Deepak Chopra and Maharishi Ayur Veda

The most financially successful of Maharishi's new products and programs were those marketed as Maharishi Ayur Veda (MAV). MAV constituted a cohesive approach to health whose overarching principle affirmed that perfect health is achieved when the forces of body and mind are brought into balance. MAV literature explained that classical texts of Ayur Veda caution that to treat a patient effectively, the physician must act holistically. Every person has three aspects – consciousness, mind, and body – and TMO literature asserted it was attention to consciousness that distinguished MAV from earlier competitors, most of whom didn't prescribe meditation. Somewhat more often, but by no means as a general rule, they prescribed *yajnas*, Sanskrit-based rituals performed by Brahmin priests (in TM circles always written in the Hindi language form yagya). Though Maharishi had emphasized the benefits of yagyas earlier, his primary emphasis continued to be on meditation and the Sidhis to develop increased consciousness. When all was said and done, for Maharishi, ill-health was caused by our own "mistake of the intellect" – *pragya-aparadh* (*prajñaparadha*). We forget the underlying unity of all things in Brahman, which leads to faulty judgments regarding how to insure our health, thus causing us to fall out of accord with natural law. Reconnecting our conscious awareness to the Absolute/Brahman/ Pure Creative Intelligence was the necessary key, Maharishi argued, though holistic treatments and food supplements had value.

In describing this approach to Ayur Veda, Hari Sharma and Christopher Clark, two TM insiders, explained that Maharishi consistently privileged his belief that the basis of health is consciousness. They noted that Maharishi sought to place MAV in a larger context: "There is an inseparable, very intimate relationship between the unmanifest field of consciousness and all the manifest levels of the physiology: that is why Maharishi's Vedic Approach to Health handles the field of health primarily from the most basic area of health – the field of consciousness – through the natural approach of consciousness, Transcendental Meditation" (Sharma & Clark 1998: 6). One must adopt the "technologies of consciousness of MAV" to reboot one's system, if you will, and thereby "overcome *pragya-aparadh* – to 'restore memory' of the unified field" (Sharma & Clark 1998: 6). Maharishi, in agreement with traditional Hinduism, believed the physical universe derives from Brahman, the Absolute, and his approach to healing the body depended on that metaphysical view.

The concept of pragya-aparadh in MAV mirrored Maharishi's basic interpretation of *avidya* gleaned from Advaita Vedanta. Just as avidya or ignorance of our true Self is the cause of bondage, with jñana (knowledge of the Self) as its antidote, so pragya-aparadh is the cause of ill-health, and jñana through tapping the field of consciousness with the TM-Sidhis Program was Maharishi's antidote. To communicate to Americans how pragya-aparadh can be overcome by jñana, Maharishi employed the more familiar language of science, though often mixed with quirky terms from quantum theory. In MAV, Maharishi fused Indian medicine with Advaita philosophy as well as with Western physics. In particular, his understanding of Brahman or Ultimate Reality functioned as the linchpin between all three. Maharishi was not the first to promote direct connections between quantum theory and religion, but his unique contribution was to foster the belief that all Western sciences were merely branches of his SCI, now synonymous or closely aligned with Vedic Science, including theories of an unmanifest unified field. Consciousness was positioned as the source – and ultimately the substance – of all physical reality, and given that all reality had consciousness in common, it was reputed to be what linked them together.

In 1985, Maharishi established his World Federation for Ayur Veda, and declared 1986 to be "The Year of Maharishi's World Plan for Perfect Health." To disseminate his teachings and treatment programs, he established an institute and clinic in Lancaster, Massachusetts, appointing as its director a young Indian endocrinologist who had been chief of staff at New England Memorial Hospital outside Boston. Deepak Chopra – now Maharishi's favored protégé – would attempt to extend the nonlocal model borrowed from quantum physics to physiology, using it as a basis to explain the value of traditional Indian medicine in his bestselling book, *Quantum Healing* (1989). Chopra, soon to be a media favorite, brought Maharishi's radically changed movement back into the spotlight.

Maharishi's theory of the quantum mechanical body rested on his view that all particles and sub-particles of reality were infused with consciousness. In modern physics, the unified field is the objective reality of nature. Consciousness is understood to be a subjective experience, but Maharishi rejected this principle, claiming that the ground state of physics and the ground state of consciousness were one and the same. When he used the term unified field, he meant the unified field as amplified by Vedic Science, which therefore included both objective and subjective aspects of reality. Accepting his theory that all of creation is infused with intelligence at the quantum level, no part of the body lives apart from the rest; each molecule has consciousness and can be transformed, since all coexist in webs of relation and all depend upon Pure Creative Intelligence (then also called in the TMO the "quantum state of least excitation") for their foundation. Thus, as higher frames of consciousness shift, so will the body. For this reason, by purifying one's consciousness, Maharishi insisted, the entire body could be healed.

But strong measures must be taken to purify one's consciousness. For instance, MAV constituted a whole complex of approaches, including meditation, pulse diagnosis, diets keyed to one's body type and personality, purification techniques, yoga, music therapy, aromatherapy, and herbal remedies. Each packaged product was available to the public whether or not they meditated, although persons were strongly advised to start. The *panchakarma* purification techniques included massage and stimulation of *marmas* (energy points in the body), healing oils, and cleansing enemas. Health would be achieved when the forces of the body and mind came into balance with pure consciousness dominating over all. For publicity's sake, attractive color catalogs and brochures displaying products and services rolled off the MIU presses.

A necessary first step to health was diagnosing the patient's mind and body type. The three fundamental principles of physical manifestation or *doshas* (*vata, pitta* and *kapha*) influence health and govern all the activities of one's mind and body, and in MAV their description did not stray far from the common Indian interpretation. Marmas, however, were understood by Maharishi in a unique sense as connecting points between the mind and body, "where consciousness becomes the material structure of the quantum mechanical body" (Sharma & Clark 1998: 121). By gently stimulating the 108 classical marma points with the appropriate Maharishi-approved, dosha-specific oil, energy blockages could be reduced and the flow of energy and intelligence, or proper consciousness, could be reestablished throughout the body.

A final philosophical innovation of MAV occurred at the hand of Dr. Anthony Nader, the Lebanese neuroscientist who first became Maharishi's favorite during the 1980 Vedic Science assembly in Delhi. According to Maharishi's website, Nader "discovered that the human physiology is a direct, material reflection of the field of consciousness, the field traditionally known as Veda, which in the language of modern physics is the Unified Field of all the Laws of Nature." The significance of Nader's discovery, according to a movement missive of May, 2001 (and a position still iterated on movement websites), was that "through proper education, every individual can have direct access to the Unified Field – the source of all the laws of nature governing the Universe – in the simplest form of human awareness."[3] And most crucially, "Access to this Unified Field brings mastery over Natural Law."[4] Nader had painstakingly – but without any academic knowledge of Sanskrit – linked forty aspects of the Vedic corpus to forty qualities of natural law, and to forty expressions of human physiology. Thus, for example, the text of the *Sama Veda* was purported to have the quality of the natural law of "flowing wakefulness," and its expression in physiology is the sensory system (Reddy & Egenes 2002: 25). According to MAV, we are all "living, breathing, talking embodiments of Veda – a storehouse of pure knowledge, pure intelligence, pure orderliness, happiness, and organizing power" (Reddy & Egenes 2002: 26).

Tony Nader's *Human Physiology: Expression of Veda and the Vedic Literature* (1994) was published by the TMO as the culminating philosophy of a panoply of products and the capstone of Maharishi's vision, for it was the scientific discovery that revealed the ultimate truth – unity in diversity and diversity in unity. Though the book is generally inscrutable and grandiose in its claims, Nader's theories were defended by Deepak Chopra in his role as Maharishi's ambassador of Ayur Veda. And just as Maharishi had eliminated the need for a guru-to-student transmission of the mantra by training thousands of TM initiators, he created a simplified system of body typing presided over by a core of *vaidyas* (Ayur Veda physicians) trained at his Maharishi Vedic universities, based in India at Katni, Bhopal, Indore, Ujjain, and Jabalpur. All Western MAV physicians were allopathic doctors who received special MAV training with qualified vaidyas from India. Patients were urged to travel to special centers, such as that located in the Maharishi Vedic City near Fairfield, for professional guidance, and thereby improve their quality of life by adopting Maharishi's many services and specialized products. For TM insiders, the days of "no change of lifestyle" or "one simple technique" were over. They were now pressured to accept, and pay for, recommended treatments.

Maharishi institutionalized a monopoly of Ayur Veda medicine based on a new paradigm: it was a traditional science, yet supposedly verifiable under the

---

[3] Quoted from a movement flyer issued to TM centers titled "Parliament of World Peace to be Inaugurated on June 14, 2001" (private collection).

[4] Ibid.

test of allopathic methodologies. Thus, his program was simultaneously authentic, or traditional, and cutting edge. Yet much of MAV did not look like what Indian Ayur Veda practitioners would recognize as authentic, nor mainstream allopathic doctors as science. Maharishi adopted New Age frameworks such as seminars and retreats, encouraging customers to visit luxury spas to be treated and pampered with individualized attention. The Raj, a luxury hotel and spa located in Maharishi Vedic City, just two miles north of Fairfield, exemplified this kinder, gentler entrepreneurial approach. The Raj offered oil treatments, massages, body typing and more, even among those who did not accept Maharishi's TM or its attendant philosophy. In this sense, MAV was involved with a less insider audience than Maharishi's earlier products, leading to issues of branding and quality control of products.

Recall that during the *Malnak* v. *Yogi* case in New Jersey, a two-page memorandum had been sent to all TMO departments regarding proper use of the term "Transcendental Meditation." Now the World Plan Executive Council (WPEC) was in the process of seeking to register as "service marks" all terms identifying movement activities, and by associating these terms with the WPEC's services, people enrolling in programs could be assured they were coming from the same source. Maharishi's way to take advantage of an avid consumer base, while preserving his control of a specific interpretation of Ayur Vedic medicine, was to develop a service marked and franchised model of branding, appending his own name to each and every aspect of his product line. Related to this move, the establishment of Maharishi brand products signaled a clear break from his earlier tendency to attribute all credit to his guru, Swami Brahmananda. Now the focus was on Maharishi himself, and the urge to control his products and programs was shown forcefully in the eventual fate of Deepak Chopra. A protégé of rare talents, Chopra was an incredible asset – arguably greater than those who had come before, including Charlie Lutes, Jerry Jarvis, Bevan Morris, Larry Domash, or any other highly favored spokesperson. Chopra could speak with health professionals or television audiences with equal ease and was as much at home in the West as he was in his native Delhi. He quickly established MAV as the most successful of the TMO's programs. Along the way, he had gained fame of his own, eventually becoming a darling of *Yoga Journal*, for example, and a close personal friend of Elizabeth Taylor and Oprah Winfrey. He was then, and continues to be, charismatic and compelling. But as Chopra's star brightened, other stars in the TM firmament dimmed in comparison, which sometimes led to conflict.

Chopra respected Maharishi but he increasingly wished for greater control of his own career and message, sometimes bristling at the institutional need to defend Nader's views as definitive of Ayur Veda.

According to Chopra, a showdown with Maharishi occurred in 1993, at Maharishi's recently established residence in Vlodrop, Holland. "Maharishi asked everyone to leave his room except me. Maharishi said to me, 'Everyone tells me you are competing with me.'" Chopra said he was stricken by this news and told Maharishi he would never do that – then, after a moment, he added, "Probably it would be best for me to leave the Movement." Chopra observed that Maharishi became very sweet then, and said, "'Whatever decision would be best for you.' . . .The whole thing lasted maybe two minutes. So I left the movement."[5]

On July 16, 1993, the Maharishi National Council of the Age of Enlightenment wrote to the few TM centers still remaining to confirm that Chopra had left the fold, adding to the missive, "Accordingly, we should discontinue promoting him, his courses, tapes, and books. [. . .] This is extremely important for the purity of the teaching."[6] Here we again see loyalty to Maharishi cast as essential to the purity of the teaching. At the very same time, when Maharishi was most worried about his brand, he also called for avoiding courses taught by Sri Sri Ravi Shankar. As was the case for Sri Sri, Chopra's teachings in the years just ahead contained the same information they had before he left the TMO. Without Maharishi's label or control, however, questions of compromised purity in the TMO arose, although they tended to be issues of autocracy rather than pedagogy.

In the 1990s, and the first decade of the twenty-first century, selling Maharishi's entire Ayur Veda package to Americans was a challenge, partially because the explanations, although consistent, were complicated, unappealing, and often indecipherable. MAV represented itself, and still does, as the entirety of the Ayur Veda tradition, thus rejecting diversity in Ayur Veda, an exclusionary tendency anathema to many Americans interested in such practices. Those people whom Maharishi elevated were given titles that many found outlandish and peculiar, leading to overall public skepticism about MAV and Maharishi's organization. For example, following Chopra's eviction, Maharishi appointed Tony Nader not only the new director of MAV but also the Maharaja Nader Raam, the sovereign ruler of Maharishi's utopia, the Global Country of World Peace, protected by an invincible shield generated by thousands of yogic flyers. Where Chopra had taken pains not to chain himself to the Hindu tradition of Ayur Veda because he wanted to broaden his appeal for an American audience, King Nader Raam – who underwent a Vedic coronation ceremony in which he was literally given his weight in gold – resolved to link quantum healing to the Vedas.

---

[5] The original interview, which once appeared on the TM website trancenet, is now offline.

[6] From an internal memo issued by the National Headquarters, private collection.

9 Suspicious Science and Trouble in Paradise

A consistent strategy of the TMO beginning around 1970 was to distance itself from spirituality and religion by emphasizing TM's scientifically endorsed health benefits. Transcendental Meditation, the organization maintained, was not a spiritual practice but a scientifically proven technique for reducing stress. In this regard, it is indeed true that TM is restful and that rest is beneficial to health. But it is also true that the TMO has a long history of overstating its legitimation by science (see, e.g., Cowan & Bromley 2008).

As early as 1974, Dr. Harrison Pope Jr., currently chair of psychiatry Harvard Medical School, asserted that the TMO had "more than once endangered its reputation among educated people by prematurely broadcasting scientific findings of tentative caliber" (Pope 1974: 37). Grandiose claims of TM's effectiveness have been challenged repeatedly by the scientific community, although that is rarely acknowledged by the TMO. These claims have inadvertently revealed more about the TMO's religious zeal than proof of its programs' efficacy.

To scientifically demonstrate its value, the TMO launched a $6 million project in Washington, DC, flooding the nation's capital in summer 1993 with 5,000 TMers who attempted to reduce the rate of violent crime by generating the Maharishi Effect. John Hagelin, a movement wunderkind with a doctorate in physics from Harvard, spearheaded the project, announcing during a press conference at its inception that having thousands of meditators practicing together would cause a "unified superstring field" predicted to reduce violent crime by 20 percent over the following two months. But according to an outside observer, "the weeks that followed [Hagelin's first press conference] seemed like something out of an old mad-scientist movie – an experiment that had gone horribly wrong. Each Monday morning, the *Washington Post* would tally the gruesome weekend slayings in the city. ... The murder rate for those two months reached a level unmatched before or since" (Park 2000: 29–30).

When the project ended, Hagelin admitted that the crime rate had indeed escalated, attributed the change to the unusually high temperatures that summer. The next year, however, he asserted that violent crime had in fact dropped (Park 2000). The TMO maintains a strict silence concerning the fact that most studies supporting TM's benefits have been conducted by TM scientists. It also continues to publish the highly disputable claim that Hagelin's project reduced violent crime in Washington, DC, during the summer of 1993. Hagelin is today the leader of the TMO in the United States.

By overstating its claims of scientific validation, the TMO's strategy generally backfired during the 1990s, reducing its credibility with the public while also reducing its trustworthiness for many TMers. True believers in the movement embraced studies such as Hagelin's as proof that the Age of Enlightenment was right around the corner, but others felt betrayed and misled. The fracture line between these two camps generally depended upon depth of commitment to Maharishi's vision and mission. True believers of the insider camp didn't bother to analyze the details, while mainstream meditators of the audience cult variety simply walked away.

We've previously noted the broad division between casual TMers drawn from the general public, who learned TM as they may have learned yoga or Tai-Chi at their local YMCA (i.e., without any acceptance of an underlying belief system), and those far fewer in number (perhaps only 10,000 to 15,000 during the 1990s) who are TM insiders. Many of these insiders were concentrated in either Fairfield, Iowa; Seelisberg, Switzerland; Voldrop, Holland; or Noida, India. Historian Elizabeth De Michelis describes this division between casual and committed as representing early TM and late TM (De Michelis 2005: 187–8), and it's easy to see why. Prior to 1977 and the movement's turn inward, there was a vast group of meditators who began during the Merv Wave – when even insiders only practiced TM – in contrast to the later period of the movement when the Sidhis and Ayur Veda treatment programs were added. While there is a chronological division to be noted, there also was from the very beginning of the movement a separation between insiders seeking spiritual enlightenment, deeply embracing Maharishi's transplanted Hindu philosophy, and those for whom, as De Michelis tells us, the "doctrinal aspects of the teachings [were] mostly rudimentary" (De Michelis 2005: 188). Though it is certainly true that Maharishi's core followers embraced an expanded understanding of Vedic Science after the advent of the Sidhis program, a division between insiders and ordinary TMers of the Stark and Bainbridge audience cult variety has existed throughout the movement's history. The willingness to accept whatever Maharishi and his officials have claimed has consistently been higher among insiders than among casual TMers. For the latter, there has been little participation with the organization and scant acceptance, or even understanding, of Maharishi's philosophy. For the former, however, their practice has often been so deep as to constitute a religious commitment, in that it generates meaning, purpose, and – in the Ideal Villages or among those true believers outside those communities – a sense of shared identity. This brings us directly to the question: Is TM a religious practice? The TMO states in all of its literature that it is not, but the fact of the matter is far more nuanced.

TMO lectures and publications – for example, Robert Roth's *TM–Transcendental Meditation* (2011) – assert that the practice is not religious, does not require a religious commitment, can be practiced by anyone of any faith, and does not demand a change of lifestyle. However, the veracity of these claims depends directly on the group of TMers being referenced. It is true that casual meditators may practice TM without changing their lifestyle or challenging their religion – if they ignore the implications of the puja ceremony (conducted in Sanskrit, a language most of them don't understand) and believe that their mantra is a "meaningless sound." But for TM insiders there was great acceptance of Maharishi's Advaita Vedanta philosophy, informing the central concerns of their lives; the practice of TM was set inside that understanding. Functioning like most religions, Maharishi's SCI provided a core of meaning and purpose for insiders based on a comprehensive view of reality and their place within it. Furthermore, this view included not only metaphysical elements in resonance with Advaita Vedanta but also a range of daily practices linked through those elements to the Hindu mainstream, including even how they should construct their houses (Lowe 2010). Unquestionably, the worldview of TM insiders was, and continues to be, religious in both the usual and academic senses of the term. Moreover, it is specifically a variety of Neo-Hinduism.

The division between those who accepted TM lightly and those who adopted Maharishi's entire worldview has often led to charges of cult-like activity against the TMO, based on the idea that the movement seeks converts for its reputedly real purpose of using meditation as an entry level to Hindu indoctrination. Examples of the anticult outlook abound on the Internet (e.g., see the archives of TM-EX online) and in several books. These include not only those mentioned previously but also Aryeh Siegel's critique, *Transcendental Deception* (2018), the apostate memoir *Greetings from Utopia Park* by Claire Hoffman (2016), *Robes of Silk Feet of Clay* by Judith Bourque (2010), covering her alleged clandestine love affair with Maharishi, and *The Maharishi Effect, A Personal Journey Through the Movement that Transformed American Spirituality* by Geoff Gilpin (2006). However, deeper analysis suggests that the TMO's policy of hiding TM's links with Hinduism are mostly innocent of the desire to generate conversions, deriving from the organization's original desire of getting people to meditate and then simply allowing meditation's influence to steer them in the right direction. Therefore, the history of the movement does not support the charge that new meditators were or have been subjected to strong pressures to assimilate into the relatively small group who accepted Maharishi's Neo-Hindu religion. Casual TMers have not been coerced into the fold – indeed, somewhat ironically they continue to form the largest division in the TM movement today. For mainstream TMers in the West, TM is not a religion. The TMO has positioned its claim of not being a religious organization by focusing public attention on mainstream TMers, often visible as celebrity meditators. The hidden agenda, however, is that its insiders most definitely have been involved with a religion since the very beginning. Cynthia Humes has wryly observed, "When is a path to enlightenment, which sponsors rituals to deities and is based on meditation that deploys the names of gods, not a religion?" (Humes 2005: 73)

* * *

In the mid-1990s, community members of Fairfield's Ideal Village most certainly fulfilled Stark and Bainbridge's criteria for a full-blown cult movement, including the fact that the group accepted a "much more elaborate package of compensators, including the most general compensators based on supernatural assumptions," along with the social rewards dependent upon "committed membership" (Bainbridge & Stark 2005: 64). But it's important to note that even among those who embraced TM religiously, there was a spectrum of commitment ranging from profound faith to provisional acceptance – not unlike what occurs in all religions. Furthermore, the Ideal Village included believers who could be described as the loyal opposition; they generally accepted Maharishi's worldview but nevertheless had a few concerns or quibbles – a circumstance we again find in other religions.

This spectrum of faith and allegiance in the Fairfield community of the mid-1990s gained a specific character due to increased tension between TM officials and the broader community of insiders. Specifically, the TMO's ideal position – used to identify its truest believers – was that insiders should embrace Maharishi's teachings fully, participate in his programs exclusively, and obey his officials unquestioningly. This position was on full display when journalist Michael D'Antonio visited MIU in 1992, prompting him to remark that he was observing a cult rather than a culture (D'Antonio 1992: 286).

This stance of TMO officials and others among the truest believers formed one end of the spectrum for insiders. The opposite pole was defined by the loyal opposition, who expressed different criticisms of the movement. These objections included disapproval of the movement's promotion of questionable scientific support for its programs, on the one hand, and its increasing drift toward Hinduism on the other. Additional grievances comprised the policy of TMO officials to excommunicate those who attended the programs of other gurus and their increasingly authoritarian behaviors, the lack of TMO officials' willingness to engage in open conversation or entertain criticism, and the ever-increasing costs of Ayur Veda products and treatments pushed upon the community. Finally, there were ongoing accusations that Maharishi had sometimes broken his monastic vow of celibacy, thereby challenging the assertion that his actions were spontaneously correct or uniformly moral. These criticisms divided the congregation of insiders on points of both ideology and practice, with true believers often galvanized in their faith by the so-called false claims of detractors, even as those detractors became convinced that true believers were falling into groupthink.

By the mid-1990s, one-quarter to one-third of the estimated 10,000 residents of Fairfield were TMers, but they had no voice in the direction of their organization. TMO officials left no room for constructive criticism, holding the attitude that disgruntled insiders should either get onboard or get out. After all, nobody was preventing them from leaving. This attitude only created further ire among detractors. They had given most of their adult lives to Maharishi's movement; they hoped they could help move it in a better direction if given a measure of representation. Why wasn't that allowed? In the late 1990s, the vast majority of TMers in Fairfield had been meditating regularly for more than twenty-five years. One consequence of this fact was that some had run out of patience with the idea that they would soon achieve enlightenment. Perhaps it was time to reassess the efficacy of the movement's programs and authority. They were approaching middle age; they were mostly loyal to the TMO but also seasoned in their views, wishing for their concerns to be heard. The TM insider who lived in Fairfield for many years and wrote the unpublished memoir mentioned much earlier, observed,

> in our community of a couple of thousand spiritually minded adherents, there remained the good and the bad. [But] genuine qualities one would associate with the expansion of consciousness and increased spirituality were not always demonstrated. What does this say about developing higher states of consciousness? This has perplexed me for years. In Fairfield it is a topic that cries out for some honest assessment.

Because many TMers agreed with this sentiment, a series of initiatives arose aimed at generating open discussion. One of the more thoughtful early efforts was launched by the late L. B. Shriver (d. 2013) on March 4, 1993, in the form of a weekly newspaper titled *Survival in Paradise*. The paper – containing mainly supportive observations and recommendations – was quickly banned from the MIU campus. After repeated attempts to put the newspaper back on shelves failed, it became clear to Shriver, and many in town, that TM officials preferred censorship over open dialogue.

Additional efforts in the 1990s and early 2000s were likewise unsuccessful. In 2001, Rick Archer launched the website *Fairfield Life* with the same hopes as Shriver, but his effort gleaned the same result. Archer was contacted by the Department for the Development of Consciousness, or DEVCO, a branch of the local TMO that accepted payments for Town Super Radiance (meditators who lived in town but practiced in the domes) and issued identity badges for entry into the domes. Archer related in a phone conversation that he was interrogated by DEVCO presumably because he and his wife had attended a lecture given by Ammachi, a female guru often called the Hugging Saint. At the same time, he thought it a suspicious coincidence that his TSR badge was revoked less than two weeks after he began hosting *Fairfield Life*.

Movement crackdowns continued, inciting both deeper pledges of loyalty and departures from the fold. Over time, the concerns of one long-time TMer led her and her family to leave Fairfield, and soon after she attended Goddard College in Vermont. She came to realize she had once accepted a blinkered view. "What I found in the first semester was that while immersion in this belief system may have had its value, I had allowed my thoughts and mental tendencies to fall into a pattern. This pattern represented the voluntary acceptance of dogma," she wrote in her unpublished memoir.

Her comments are typical of many who left the TMO in the 1990s. They may not have withdrawn in anger, but they were now either too discouraged or too open-minded to participate. Some would leave Fairfield and some would stay simply because their homes were there. In other cases, detractors would keep a low profile and participate when and if they saw fit – often pursuing other types of programs and treatments along the way. In fact, by the end of the millennium, Fairfield was renowned as a haven for New Agers in the United States, triggering an influx of gurus and alternative spiritual programs. (For a detailed look at the community of Fairfield, see Weber 2014.) This flood of outside programs was ignored by TM officials at first, but that policy changed in 1994 (mostly likely due to Chopra's exit), with the charge that those seeking other gurus were disloyal and therefore would be excluded from access to the domes. A disinformation campaign arose specifically against Sri Sri Ravi Shankar, with anonymous letters and notices posted in TM venues spreading untruths, denying any link between him and Maharishi, and warning meditators not to associate with him.

Detractors were upset with judgments of who and what constituted heterodoxy. Since most insiders had spent more years studying with Maharishi than he had spent with his own guru, they felt they had a clear understanding of his teachings. They could attend lectures by other gurus and seek Ayur Veda treatments elsewhere while deciding for themselves if they were on or off the program. One enticement in that direction was that treatments, tonics, and cures offered by doctors, astrologers, and therapists outside the movement were often far less expensive than Maharishi's brand. Related to this fact, some TMers were, in a sense, actually priced out of complying with Maharishi's directives. They had accepted his views regarding how to improve their health and facilitate their spiritual growth but, ironically, couldn't afford to purchase his products, seeking their equivalents elsewhere. Paradoxically, they went rogue simply because it was their only means of complying with Maharishi's directives.

10 After Maharishi

In 1992, Dr. John Hagelin, a physicist at MIU, appeared on the ballots of forty-six states as a candidate for the US presidency; he would run again in 1996 and 2000 (Cowan & Bromley 2008: 48). In all cases, his platform was inspired by Maharishi's Vedic Science. After the failure of these attempts at steering the American government in the right direction, Maharishi announced on October 7, 2000, that motivated by "the persistent failure of national administrations throughout human history, and the pressing need for a more effective system of administration," he was abandoning secular processes and inaugurating instead the Global Country of World Peace (Humes 2005: 78, endnote 41). Maharishi's move away from what he characterized in an interview with Larry King as "damn democracy" (CNN Larry King Weekend 2002) toward the more controllable policies of his Global Country, would allow him to appoint his cabinet in line with his own theories of meritocracy.

What sort of country was (and is) the Global Country of World Peace? According to its website, the "domain of the Global Country of World Peace is CONSCIOUSNESS," and its authority is in the invincible power of "Natural Law" (Global Country of World Peace 2022). Maharishi explained to Larry King that this virtual domain would operate according to the "constitution of the universe," which is none other than "total natural law" (CNN Larry King Weekend 2002). The Global Country was, in Maharishi's scheme, the sovereign realm of Brahman/Absolute Being/Pure Creative Intelligence and the unified field that, he argued, underlies all reality. Maharishi selected Tony Nader to preside over this amorphous country. Nader was subsequently crowned "Maharaja Nader Raam," while thirty-three lesser rajas, including John Hagelin, were crowned along with him. The nascent Global Country also issued a currency in 2002 (the Ram is equal to US$10), allowing TM insiders to buy support for their virtual kingdom by investing in its government. One key project of that government was to finance sustainable, communal farms in the world's poorest countries; another was to build Peace Palaces in the major cities of the world. Eventually, modest Peace Palaces were designed and built in four or five countries. MIU Press continues to offer a book titled *How to Build a Peace Palace* (Hartmann 2013).

Readying the Peace Palaces was a cardinal concern of the Global Country's initiative to hurry along a new era, termed Satya Yuga. Maharishi took steps to insure the purity of the teaching in this regard, declaring that TM teachers who hadn't taught recently (as far the TMO was aware) needed to be recertified. A March 27, 2005, memorandum, giving information about Governor Recertification Courses, noted that those governors of the Age of Enlightenment who wished to become full-time teachers in appointed Peace Palace cities would need to attend a month-long refresher, after which they would be assigned by the regional raja to enlighten as many people as possible. By requiring recertification, the TMO sought to address a number of perceived problems, with a premium placed on strengthening affiliations with the organization and controlling the brand.

Teachers dispensing TM for free or at reduced rates was no longer an option. Only certified governors could teach TM techniques. An interesting irony here may be that circumstantial evidence, gleaned from interviews with dozens of TM teachers, suggests that during this period more people may have been initiated into TM annually by initiators working outside the TMO than inside. These renegade teachers, claiming they had no respect for the TMO or its high prices (the TM course currently costs $1,000), scoffed at having to be recertified. Several argued that their knowledge of how to teach TM was equal to that of the TMO leadership, and they saw no reason to bow to authority – despite whomever Maharishi appointed as raja. One former TM teacher related during an interview that the leadership was the group compromising the purity. "When I learned [to teach TM] – and I learned directly from Maharishi, as did many others – there was not all this added mumbo-jumbo about astrology and food supplements. It was just about meditation."

For many TM insiders of the detractor camp (i.e., those who openly left the formal organization or silently kept their distance from it), the TM movement is not synonymous with the TMO, as it is for the deep insiders. For them, the TMO is a rogue organization that drifted away from the original mission, as indeed Maharishi may have as well. Conversely, the TMO claims absolute authority in all matters related to TM, a trademarked brand. Its officials cite the Robin Carlsen case and others to illustrate the problems caused by teachers acting on their own.

At approximately 7 p.m. on Tuesday, February 5, 2008, Maharishi passed away peacefully at his home in Vlodrop, Holland. His body was then flown to Allahabad, and on Tuesday, February 12, pallbearers carried his body to a specially erected platform overlooking the holy confluence of three rivers: the Ganges, the Yamuna, and the mythological Saraswati. Receiving the body were Maharishi's recently nominated successor, Maharaja Nader Raam, the other thirty-three rajas (kings), as well as the thirteen-member Global Council of Ministers. All wore white silk brocade regalia and the rajas sported golden crowns. Sri Sri Ravi Shankar also offered obeisance before the cremation, as did other celebrities gathered around, including Hollywood filmmaker David Lynch. A press release from the TMO issued the next day officially summarized what was felt to be Maharishi's legacy. Over five million people had learned

Maharishi's TM, it claimed. He had inspired research on the society-wide benefits of TM. He had revived the complete Vedic Science of ancient India, and integrated it with the latest discoveries of modern science. Most importantly, he had brought "complete knowledge" to all areas of society.

In addition to the honorific celebrations given by TM insiders, people around the world reacted to Maharishi's death by remembering his contributions. Celebrity meditators, including Paul McCartney, Howard Stern, and Jerry Seinfeld, shared their respects publicly, citing the many benefits they enjoyed from their practice of TM. News agencies reported that Maharishi was responsible for putting meditation and its rewards for health on the map, and other accolades followed. Even insiders who had become critics of the official TMO often shared in interviews that they had been saddened by Maharishi's passing. "He taught me a philosophy that has guided my life and brought me peace of mind," a former initiator informed the authors by email, "and he taught me how to quiet my mind. These are valuable gifts for which I'm eternally grateful."

After Maharishi's death, officials of the Global Country took the reins of the TMO, offering not only TM courses but also the Sidhis program and the Ayur Veda offerings. Today, however, there is one official organ of the TMO that has actually returned to Maharishi's original mission of teaching TM to as many people as possible: the David Lynch Foundation.

In 1973, Lynch had been looking into different meditation techniques when he learned about TM from his sister. Thirty years into his practice, Lynch participated in Maharishi's 2003 four-week Millionaire's Enlightenment Course in Holland, and became close to the aging guru. In July 2005, Lynch established a new charity, the David Lynch Foundation (DLF) for Consciousness-Based Education and World Peace, with Robert Roth as its director. Today, the DLF seeks to support the teaching of TM to a million school children in the United States alone, with programs in other countries as well, with a focus particularly on disadvantaged youth. Lynch's foundation portrays TM on its website in terms reminiscent of the 1970s, as a "simple technology" with no ties to religion. By linking TM to the Lynch foundation, rather than Maharishi's organization, criticisms of teaching a religious practice in public schools have been muted. "Quiet Time" is the foundation's term for TM in schools (Center for Resilience 2022), and though there have been cries of illegal behavior (e.g., in 2020, "Quiet Time" was dropped from five public high schools in Chicago on the grounds that TM is a religious practice), the program continues to enlist schools in the program. Though the intent is most certainly benevolent, the issue raised in the New Jersey court case of 1976 – that teaching TM in public schools goes against the separation of church and state – has come into play. The foundation, like the TMO in general, directs public attention toward how TM has been used by casual meditators who have ignored, or haven't realized, the Hindu content of the Maharishi's philosophy and practices. There is no possibility that TM teachers inside the DLF, or the TMO in general, aren't aware of these connections, so these pieces of information are simply left out of presentations – or worse, disavowed. Aryeh Siegel, a former TM insider, has argued: "Because it flies under the radar, TM can't acknowledge that it must withhold information about its secretive practices from parents, teachers, and school officials to gain support for its programs" (Siegel 2018: 151).

The TMO still refuses to accept the judgment of the New Jersey court or the analyses of academics today who describe the group's message as religious. The organization seems to want to hold onto the idea that practitioners can believe like Hindus and behave like Hindus and still not be Hindus. However, when one looks closely at Maharishi's core group of insiders, the more they appear like other Neo-Hindus of the export variety. "Contrary to Sai Baba," Cynthia Humes observed, "who moved from the particulars of Hindu/Indian religion to a more universalist stance, Maharishi began with a universalist stance, rooted in the technique of *samadhi* through Transcendental Meditation, and has moved to an ever more particularist stance, gradually embedding the Hindu/ Vedic religion year by year as successive unveilings of the most accurate vision of true religion" (Humes 2005: 72).

> And what of Maharishi's originally stated goals – his higher aims – to bring Cosmic Consciousness to his students and peace to the world? Though many have practiced TM for thirty-five, forty, and even fifty years, few have ever claimed to reach enlightenment and none – including Sri Sri Ravi Shankar – was ever recognized as authentic by Maharishi or the TMO. In addition, there's little evidence the world has entered an Age of Enlightenment.

Nevertheless, Maharishi seems to have sincerely hoped to be of service to humanity. TMers who left the organization tend to focus their criticisms on the hierarchy he created and allowed, his reversal of opinion about the singular efficacy of TM to improve one's life, and the increased Hinduization of his programs. These charges have helped create a general wariness in American Neo-Hinduism toward spiritual masters, reinforced by serious scandals involving other gurus. One positive effect of these schisms, scandals, and guru-debunkings may be a reduction of naiveté on the part of Americans involved with Hindu teachings. There has been a proverbial baptism by fire that has tempered the tendency toward idealization of gurus that marked Neo-Hinduism in the 1970s.

In his analysis of TM, Scientology, and other new religions, sociologist Roy Wallis observed that certain movements shared a view of humanity as perfectible. Rather than changing society, they would facilitate the transformation of individuals (Wallis 2003: 48–9). Wallis captures the tone of the early TM movement. From the start, Maharishi argued that his goal was the spiritual regeneration of humanity by means of the expansion of individual consciousness, and consciousness expansion was easily attained through TM. But as decades and decades passed by and none of the promised upgrades in individual or collective awakening transpired, how did the organization keep its utopian dream alive? Why didn't all the insiders walk away in the 1990s when they hadn't reached enlightenment?

For the casual meditators, there was no reason to keep the dream in place because they never appropriated TM on that level. For them, the goals of the practice were humble, having to do with getting rest, relieving stress, and improving health. These goals were actually achieved for many. Several interviewees reported that they continue to do TM because it feels like a refreshing nap or a chance to catch up on alone time. But for insiders, there has been a range of reactions to the failure of their hopes. Some felt deflated by not reaching Cosmic Consciousness; some felt the overall plan might have worked if more people had learned TM; and others, from deep inside the movement, continued to claim Maharishi's plan is still on the cusp of becoming realized.

Analyzing the circumstances of this last group, the deep insiders, who continue to view the TMO as synonymous with the TM movement, we find they are most characteristic not only of Bainbridge and Stark's cult movement type, but also resonant with the NRMs Bainbridge and Stark place inside a subculture-evolution model dependent upon "group interaction processes" (Bainbridge & Stark 2003: 66). Such a group, embracing utopian dreams of human perfectibility, begins its evolution when it "commits itself to the attainment of certain rewards" (Bainbridge & Stark 2003: 67). In the case of TM's deep insiders, these rewards were once – as they continue to be for many – specifically to become fully realized beings who would bring about the Age of Enlightenment. As they worked together to obtain these rewards, they exchanged other rewards in the meantime, as Bainbridge and Stark argue is common to such groups. Specifically, they gained a communal sense of identity and purpose based on a shared sense of life's true meaning, and when the TMO turned inward in the late 1970s, these less lofty benefits grew stronger.

Bainbridge and Stark argue that over time, and as members of such NRMs "progressively come to experience failure in achieving their original goals, they will gradually generate and exchange compensators" (Bainbridge & Stark 2003: 69). These compensators are described as benefits that come to stand in for the original rewards, including the deferred gratification associated with them. In the case of the deep insiders, Cosmic Consciousness did not happen, nor did utopia, but there existed a wide range of lesser benefits that were sought and enjoyed. For instance, members of the Ideal Village not only enjoyed their acquired sense of meaning based in Maharishi's philosophy, they also were rewarded with community purpose and support, with collective identity and shared norms of behavior, with constant reinforcements that they were living correctly, and even with such mundane benefits as TM-related jobs and a sense of ongoing altruism through their practice in the domes. It is also true that what might be called negative benefits were enjoyed, derived from a shared sense that outsiders – and especially those who weren't supporting Maharishi's programs – were to blame for the slow progress toward their goals. Those on the inside could salute each other while still acknowledging that the original rewards hadn't arrived. They were doing good even if the world wasn't.

There is still more that can be said. There were rewards for social climbing within the organization, including the granting of titles, positions, wealth, and corporate perks – even reaching up to the level of wearing crowns and special costumes. The point is, however, the deep insiders of the TM-based new religious movement developed rich compensators for their unattained original goals. New projects kept them busy, and as these projects were accomplished – such as construction of golden domes, Peace Palaces, and invincibility towers; relocation to the Ideal Village; travel to India and elsewhere for courses – they felt moments of achievement that increased their sense of belonging and identity, resulting for many in the satisfaction of being spiritual sojourners that continues today.

Where this NRM will go in the future bears watching. Eyewitnesses report that fewer than 300 meditators regularly attend practice in the golden domes, which seems to imply that the deepest TM insiders have either moved away from Fairfield or, like their guru, passed away, while younger replacements have not joined the organization. In that regard, the compensators that have accumulated in the TMO over the past four decades are far less likely to attract a new audience than was spiritual enlightenment and utopia promised to the original audience. Moreover, recruitment seems difficult, given mainstream culture's wariness of guru movements, and young people's general adoption of a "spiritual but not religious" outlook, which disdains authoritarian control.

What of the TM movement's future outside of the TMO? One possibility, of course, is that it will simply die out with its practitioners, as have numerous other religious movements centered on alternative treatments, cures, and therapies. Another possibility, suggested by anecdotal evidence, is that teachers of TM who have drifted away from the official organization might create one or more affiliations of their own. Thom Knoles, founder of Vedic Meditation based on TM, has argued that TM is simply the trademarked brand of a meditation practice taught in India's Shankara tradition; he and others believe that all that needs to happen is that TM teachers change the name of what they're teaching, without altering the practice in any way (Knoles 2022). Yet another possibility is that such teachers simply teach TM for free, using the same name and offering the same service, as, for instance, is already occurring in the United Kingdom. In 2000, The Meditation Trust was established as a registered charity in the United Kingdom, with "the mission of making TM available and affordable for anyone interested" (www.meditationtrust.com/). The trust is not affiliated with any other TMO and represents one branch of this broad movement to keep the practice of TM alive outside the control of Maharishi's Global Country. Time will tell which, if any, of these scenarios will dominate.

References

Aron, E. & A. Aron. (1986). *The Maharishi Effect*. Walpole, NH: Stillpoint.

Bainbridge, W. S & R. Stark (2003). "Cult Formation: Three Compatible Models." In L. L. Dawson, ed. *Cults and New Religious Movements*. Malden, MA: Blackwell, 59–70.

Barker, E. (1985). *The Sacred in a Secular Age*. Berkeley: University of California Press.

Bellah, R. N., R. Madsen, W. M. Sullivan, A. Swidler, & S. M. Tipton (1985). *Habits of the Heart*. Berkeley: University of California Press.

Bloomfield, H., M. P. Cain, D. T. Jaffe, & R. B. Kory (1974). *TM: Discovering Inner Energy and Overcoming Stress*. New York: Delacorte Press.

Borland, C. & G. Landrith (1977). "Improved Quality of City Life through the Transcendental Meditation Program: Decreased Crime Rate." In D. Orme-Johnson, & J. T. Farrow, eds. *Scientific Research on the Transcendental Meditation and TM-Sidhis Program: Collected Papers*, Volume 1. Livingston Manor, NY: MIU Press, 639–646.

Bourque, J. (2010). *Robes of Silk, Feet of Clay*. Self-published, printed in Lithuania, ISBN: 978–91–633–6278–1, www.robersofsilkfeetofclay.com.

Carlsen, R. W. (1979). *The Sunnyside Drama: the First Three Years of Enlightenment*. Victoria, B.C.: Snow Man Press.

Center for Resilience. (2022). "Quiet Time Program." David Lynch Foundation. www.davidlynchfoundation.org/schools.html.

Chopra, D. (1989). *Quantum Healing*. New York: Bantam.

Clark, G. (1975). "The TM Craze, Forty Minutes to Bliss." *Time Magazine*, 106, no. 5, 71–74.

CNN Larry King Weekend. (2002). "Interview with Maharishi Mahesh Yogi." May 12. http://transcripts.cnn.com/TRANSCRIPTS/0205/12/lklw.00.html.

Cooke de Herrera, N. (1992). *Beyond Gurus: A Woman of Many Worlds*. New Delhi: Blue Dolphin.

Cowan, D. E. & D. G. Bromley (2008). "Transcendental Meditation: The Questions of Science and Therapy." In Cowan, D. E. & D. G. Bromley. *Cults and New Religions, a Brief History*. Hoboken, NJ: Wiley Blackwell, 38–58.

Dass, R. (1971). *Be Here Now*. San Cristobal, NM: Lama Foundation.

D'Antonio, M. (1992). *Heaven on Earth: Dispatches from America's Spiritual Frontier*. New York: Crown.

Dawson, L. L. (1998). *Comprehending Cults*. Toronto: Oxford University Press.

Dawson, L. L., ed. (2003). *Cults and New Religious Movements*. Malden, MA: Blackwell.

De Michelis, E. (2005). *A History of Modern Yoga*. London: Continuum.

Denniston, D. & P. McWilliams (1975). *The TM Book: How to Enjoy the Rest of Your Life*. Allen Park, MI: Versemonger Press.

Dragemark, E. (1972). *The Way to Maharishi's Himalayas*. Stockholm: Forenede Trykkerier AS.

Driscoll, Francis G. (1972). "TM as a Secondary School Subject," in *Phi Delta Kappan*, 54: 236–7.

Ebon, M., ed. (1968), re-released in 1975). *Maharishi, the Guru*. New York: Signet Books.

Forem, J. (1973). *Transcendental Meditation*. New York: E. P. Dutton.

Gates, R. (1976). *Celebrating the Dawn*. New York: G.P. Putnam's Sons.

Gautier, F. (2008). *Guru of Joy: Sri Sri Ravi Shannkara and the Art of Living*. Temple City, CA: Hay House.

Gibson, W. (1974). *A Season in Heaven*. New York: Athenaeum.

Gilpin, G. (2006). *The Maharishi Effect: A Personal Journey Through the Movement that Transformed American Spirituality*. Toronto: Penguin Random House.

Global Country of World Peace. (2022). www.globalcountry.org/wp/.

Goldberg, P. (2010). *American Veda*. New York: Doubleday.

Goldman, R. A. (1988). *The Lives of John Lennon*. New York: William Morrow.

Hagelin, J. (1998). *Manual for a Perfect Government: How to Harness the Laws of Nature to Bring Maximum Success to Governmental Administration*. Fairfield, IA: MIU Press.

Hartmann, L.-M. (2013). *How to Build a Peace Palace*. Fairfield, IA: MIU Press.

Hoffman, C. (2016). *Greetings from Utopia Park*. San Francisco: HarperCollins.

Humes, C. A. (2005). "Maharishi Mahesh Yogi: Beyond the TM Technique." In R. A. Forsthoefel & C. A. Humes, eds. *Gurus in America*. Albany: State University of New York Press, 55–70.

Humes, C. A. (2009). "Schisms within Hindu Guru Groups: the Transcendental Meditation Movement in North America." In J. R. Lewis & S. M. Lewis, eds. *Sacred Schisms: How Religions Divide*. New York: Cambridge University Press, 287–305.

Huxley, A. (1954). *The Doors of Perception*. New York: Harper & Row.

Kanellakos, D. P. & J. S. Lukas (1974). *The Psychobiology of Transcendental Meditation: A Literature Survey*. Menlo Park, CA: W. A. Benjamin.

Knoles. T. (2022). "What Is Vedic Mediation." https://thomknoles.com/what-is-vedic-meditation/

Leary, T., R. Metzner & R. Alpert (1964). *The Psychedelic Experience.* New York: University Books.

Lewis, J. R. (2003). *Legitimating New Religions.* New Brunswick, NJ: Rutgers University Press.

Lowe, S. (2010). "The Neo-Hindu Transformation of an Iowa Town." *Nova Religio*, 13, no. 3: 81–91.

Lowe, S. (2011). "Transcendental Meditation, Vedic Science and Science." *Nova Religio*, 14, no. 4: 54–76.

Lutes, C. F. (1968) . "Preface." In M. Mahesh Yogi, *Meditations of Maharishi Mahesh Yogi.* New York: Bantam Books. The short preface can be accessed online at www.maharishiphotos.com/write3.html.

MacDonald, Ian (2005). *Revolution in the Head: The Beatles Records and the Sixties.* London: Pimlico.

Mason, P. (2014). Quotes from "Beacon Light of the Himalayas" are in *Dandi Swami*, 34. The book has no listed publisher but "Premananda," 2014, ISBN:978–0–9562228–4–8.

Mahesh Yogi, M. (1963). *The Science of Being and Art of Living.* London: George Allen & Unwin.

Mahesh Yogi, M. (1969). *On the Bhagavad-Gita.* Middlesex, UK: Penguin Books.

Maynard, A. (1968). "From Gurdjieff to Maharishi." In M. Ebon, ed. *Maharishi, the Guru.* New York: Signet Books, 125–129.

McCutchan, R. (1977). "The Social and the Celestial: Mary Douglas and Transcendental Meditation." *The Princeton Journal of Arts and Sciences*, 1: 130–163.

McWilliams, P. (1994). *LIFE 102: What to Do When Your Guru Sues You.* Los Angeles: Prelude Press.

Miller, J. M. (2006). *A Wave in the Ocean: Maharishi Mahesh Yogi, Transcendental Meditation, Mallory & Me.* Morrisville, NC: Lulu Press.

Nader, A. (1994). *Human Physiology: Expression of Veda and the Vedic Literature.* Fairfield, IA: Maharishi Vedic University Press.

Nattier, J. (1997). "Buddhism Comes to Main Street." *Wilson Quarterly*, 21, no. 2: 72–80. http://archive.wilsonquarterly.com/essays/buddhism-comes-main-street.

Oates Jr., Robert. 1976 *Celebrating the Dawn.* New York: G. P. Putnam's Sons

Olson, H., R. & T. Olson. (2001). *His Holiness Maharishi Mahesh Yogi: A Living Saint for the New Millennium.* Schenectady, NY: Samhita Productions.

Orme-Johnson, D. W., M. C. Dillbeck, & J. B. Bousquet. (1978). "The World Peace Project: An Experimental Analysis of Achieving Peace through the

Maharishi Technology of the Unified Field." In David Orme-Johnson & John T. Farrow, eds., *Collected Papers*, Volume 4. Fairfield, IA: MIU Press (Published simultaneously in Germany by Maharishi European Research University Press).

Orme-Johnson D. W., R. K. Wallace, M. C. Dillbeck, O. Ball, & C. N. Alexander. (1981). "Behavioral correlates of EEG phase coherence." Paper presented at the annual Convention of the American Psychological Association, Los Angeles, August, 1981. Reprinted in David Orme-Johnson, ed. *Collected Papers*, Volume 2. Fairfield, IA: MIU Press.

Paglia, C. (1990). *Sexual Personae*. New York: Vintage.

Park, R. (2000). *Voodoo Science: the Road from Foolishness to Fraud*. Oxford, UK: Oxford University Press.

Perry, C. (1984). *The Haight-Ashbury*. New York: Vintage Books.

Pope, H. Jr. (1974). *The Road East*. Boston: Beacon Press.

Reddy, K. & L. Egenes. (2002). *Conquering Chronic Disease Through Maharishi Vedic Medicine*. Schenectady, NY: Samhita Productions.

Robbins, J. & D. Fischer (1973). *Tranquility Without Pills*. New York: Bantam.

Robins, A. & J. A. Himber (1976). *Dawn of a New Age: The TM Program and Enlightenment*. Berkeley, CA: Medallion Books.

Roth, Robert (2011). *TM – Transcendental Meditation*. Fairfield, IA: Maharishi University of Management Press.

Russell, P. (1976). *The TM Technique*. London: Routledge & Kegan Paul.

Selye, H. (1974). "Forward." In H. Bloomfield, M. P. Cain, D. T. Jaffe, & R. B. Kory. *TM: Discovering Inner Energy and Overcoming Stress*. New York: Delacorte Press.

Sharma, H. & C. Clark. (1998). *Contemporary Ayurveda*. New York: Churchill Livingston.

Siegel, A. (2018). *Transcendental Deception*. Los Angeles: Janreg Press.

TM-EX Newsletter archive (1990–4) http://minet.org/TM-EX/index.html.

TM in Court. (1978). Berkeley, CA: Spiritual Counterfeits Project.

Trout, P. (2001). *Eastern Seeds, Western Soil: Three Gurus in America*. Mountain View, CA: Mayfield.

Wallace, R. K. & H. Benson (1972). "The Physiology of Meditation." *Scientific American* 226: 84–90.

Wallis, R. 1984). *The Elementary Forms of New Religious Life*. London: Routledge and Kegan Paul.

Wallis, R. (2003). "Three Types of New Religious Movements." In L. Dawson ed., *Cults and New Religious Movements*. Malden, MA: Blackwell, 36–58.

Watts, A. (1965). *The Joyous Cosmology*. New York: New World Library.

Weber, J. (2014). *Transcendental Meditation in America: How a New Age Movement Remade a Small Town in Iowa.* Iowa City: University of Iowa Press.

Weldon, J. (1976). *The Transcendental Explosion.* Irvine, CA: Harvest House.

White, J. (1976). *Everything You Want to Know About TM.* New York: Pocket Books.

Wilkins, Charles (1785). *The Bhagavad Gita: Dialogues of Krishna and Arjun.* London: Nourse.

Williamson, L. (2010). *Transcendent in America.* New York: New York University Press.

Winquist, W. T. (1976). "The Transcendental Meditation Program and Drug Abuse: A Retrospective Study." In David Orme-Johnson & John T. Farrow, eds. *Scientific Research on the Transcendental Meditation and TM-Sidhis Program: Collected Papers*, Volume 1, pp.494–497. Livingston Manor, NY: MIU Press.

Acknowledgments

The authors would particularly like to thank Bob Brigante, Allen Cobb, Nancy Cooke de Herrera, Gemma Cowhig, Shannon Dickson, Chuck Shipman, Larry Domash, Charlie Donahue, LaVergne Dunn, Rick Archer, Scott Lowe, Ty Gale, Claudia Turnbull, Michael Broderick, Philip Goldberg, Robert Gordon, Paul Hart, Debbie Jarvis, Jerry Jarvis, Mitchell Kapor, John Knapp, Laura Spear, Curtis Mailloux, Paul Mason, Vincent P. McCarthy, Pat Ryan, Gene Requa, and L. B. Shriver for their time and thoughtful comments.

New Religious Movements

Founding Editor

†James R. Lewis
Wuhan University

The late James R. Lewis was Professor of Philosophy at Wuhan University, China. He currently edits or co-edits four book series, is the general editor for the *Alternative Spirituality and Religion Review*, and the associate editor for the *Journal of Religion and Violence*. His publications include *The Cambridge Companion to Religion and Terrorism* (Cambridge University Press 2017) and *Falun Gong: Spiritual Warfare and Martyrdom* (Cambridge University Press 2018).

Series Editor

Rebecca Moore
San Diego State University

Rebecca Moore is Emerita Professor of Religious Studies at San Diego State University. She has written and edited numerous books and articles on Peoples Temple and the Jonestown tragedy. Publications include *Beyond Brainwashing: Perspectives on Cult Violence* (Cambridge University Press 2018) and *Peoples Temple and Jonestown in the Twenty-First Century* (Cambridge University Press 2022). She is reviews editor for *Nova Religio*, the quarterly journal on new and emergent religions published by the University of California Press.

About the Series

Elements in New Religious Movements go beyond cult stereotypes and popular prejudices to present new religions and their adherents in a scholarly and engaging manner. Case studies of individual groups, such as Transcendental Meditation and Scientology, provide in-depth consideration of some of the most well known, and controversial, groups. Thematic examinations of women, children, science, technology, and other topics focus on specific issues unique to these groups. Historical analyses locate new religions in specific religious, social, political, and cultural contexts. These examinations demonstrate why some groups exist in tension with the wider society and why others live peaceably in the mainstream. The series highlights the differences, as well as the similarities, within this great variety of religious expressions. To discuss contributing to this series please contact Professor Moore, remoore@sdsu.edu.

Cambridge Elements ‗

New Religious Movements

Elements in the Series

Lightning Source UK Ltd.
Milton Keynes UK
UKHW020622010223
416280UK00021B/303

9 781009 365499